THE
SAUSAGE
BOOK

THE SAUSAGE BOOK

The complete guide to making, cooking & eating sausages

Nick Sandler & Johnny Acton

Photography by Cristian Barnett

Kyle Books

This edition published in 2011 by
Kyle Books
23 Howland Street, London WIT 4AY
www.kylebooks.com

First published in Great Britain in 2010 by Kyle Cathie Ltd

10 9 8 7 6 5 4 3 2

ISBN 978-1-85626-924-7

Project editor: Jenny Wheatley
Copy editor: Salima Hirani
Photographer: Cristian Barnett
Designer: Georgia Vaux
Food stylist: Linda Tubby
Props stylist: Liz Belton
Editorial assistant: Elanor Clarke
Production: Gemma John

A Cataloguing In Publication record for this title is available from the British Library.

Acknowledgements

The authors would like to thank:

Michael and Joan Little for rent-free use of their pig sties, Angelina Harrison for corn dog inspiration, Weschenfelder & Sons for essential sausage making equipment, Grassmere Farm for pork supplies, Linda Tubby (the best food stylist in the business), Bocaddon Farm for high quality veal, Tim Wilson and his staff at The Ginger Pig farms in Yorkshire, Bod Webster and the Chapolard family in the Lot et Garonne, Gref-Völsings in Frankfurt, Casa Riera Ordeix in Catalunya, Jo McSween in Edinburgh and our long-suffering wives Lai and Percy. Johnny would not like to thank the postman who plonked a bunch of mail into the improvised smoker in front of his house despite it belching smoke at the time.

Websites offering sausage related products:

www.scobiesdirect.com
www.weschenfelder.co.uk
www.designasausage.com
www.sausagemaking.org
www.sausagemaker.com

Nick Sandler is the Creative Chef for Pret A Manger, and therefore responsible for countless lunches on a daily basis. He is also a freelance development chef, creating new dishes for delis and supermarkets.

Johnny Acton is a writer and amateur pig keeper who has authored books on topics ranging from the role of high altitude ballooning in the Space Race (*The Man Who Touched the Sky*) to economics for kids (*DK Economy*).

Together Nick and Johnny have written five books for Kyle Cathie Ltd – *Soup, Mushroom, Preserved, Duchy Originals Cookbook* and *The Branded Cookbook.*

CONTENTS

The Joy of Sausages — 6

History of the Sausage — 8

The Ultimate Sausage Experience — 9

Types of Sausage — 10

Making Your Own Sausages — 12

How to Make Fresh Sausages — 14

Other Fresh Sausages — 16

How To Make Cured Sausages — 18

Other Cured Sausages — 20

How To Make Precooked Sausages — 22

Other Precooked Sausages — 24

How To Smoke Sausages — 26

How To Make Blood Sausages — 28

FRESH SAUSAGES — 30

PRECOOKED SAUSAGES — 74

CURED SAUSAGES — 114

SKINLESS SAUSAGES & SAUSAGE MEAT — 142

SAUSAGE COUSINS — 160

FISH & VEGGIE SAUSAGES — 176

Sausages A–Z — 188

Index — 191

THE JOY OF SAUSAGES

The world, it is fair to say, is in love with the sausage. For large swathes of the Earth's population, life without hot dogs, chorizos and salamis is scarcely imaginable. The Chinese would be miserable without their lap cheong, Germany boasts over 1,200 varieties of sausage and even the Inuit get in on the act, inserting pieces of whale blubber into sections of intestine and air-drying or smoking the resultant packages.

So what is it about sausages that appeals to us so deeply? Well for one thing, people have been making them for millennia. Hunter gatherers, whose lifestyle approximates to that of our distant ancestors, often chop up parts of their kills and roast them in the animals' stomachs (the original haggis). Sausages are mentioned in Homer's *Odyssey* and were so closely associated with riotous Roman fertility festivals that the Christian authorities banned them for six centuries. They might as well not have bothered, of course – Italians would no more give up their sausages than pasta – but the fact the Catholic Church even tried is a testament to the power of the sausage.

Tradition is clearly an important part of our devotion to sausages. They are also highly convenient, fresh ones being easy to cook and cured or smoked ones having long shelf lives. But the ultimate attraction of chopped ingredients stuffed into edible skins must lie in the things themselves. Freud would have had a few theories about that, but for our money it's all about taste. The processes of sausage making allow tastes to be melded in unique and harmonious ways, while the skins form barriers that permit fascinating transformations to take place beneath, and also keep the contents succulent.

We could and will go on all day about the wonders of sausages, but a couple more of their advantages deserve special mention. First, they are economical. Sausages allow you to prepare delicious meals without breaking the bank. Even top-quality examples (the only kind we'd advise you to buy) are eminently affordable compared with conventional cuts of meat. Second, being almost universal, sausages offer an excellent and non-threatening way to explore the world's diverse tastes and culinary traditions. If you get the sausage bug, you will never run out of new avenues to explore.

HISTORY OF THE SAUSAGE

Attempting to pinpoint the origin of something as universal as the sausage is a losing battle, but we can certainly trace the trajectory of its history in the West. The earliest written instructions for sausage making were etched onto a clay tablet in Sumeria around 5,000 years ago. The most significant sausage enthusiasts of the ancient world, however, were the Romans, who brought the art of stuffing minced meat into casings to every corner of their vast empire. They also provided many European languages with their vocabulary for the delicacies: the words sausage, *salsiccia* (Italian), *saucisson* (French) and *salsichon* (Spanish) are all derived from the Latin *salsisium,* which literally means 'something salted'.

As this etymology implies, sausage making prior to the modern era was primarily about meat preservation (salt is a powerful preservative which works by depriving foods of moisture, thereby impeding the growth of harmful bacteria). This was extremely important prior to the advent of refrigeration. It is easy to imagine Roman legionnaires sustaining themselves in far-flung parts of the empire by munching on primitive salamis and pepperonis. But the addition of salt wasn't the only way to give sausages long shelf lives. They could be dried, smoked, infused with antibacterial herbs and spices or any combination of these techniques.

The methods of sausage production that became prevalent in any European region depended on its geography and climate. Around the Mediterranean, conditions favoured the production of air-dried sausages, particularly in winter when the weather wasn't too hot. In the damper environments of Northern and Eastern Europe, 'keeping' sausages were typically smoked to provide additional insurance against spoilage. Meanwhile, in every area, sausages were flavoured with locally popular herbs and spices, such as caraway in Germany, ground pimento in Spain and fennel seed in Italy.

Fresh sausages have existed for at least as long as cured ones, but in many areas they were less important economically because of the preservation imperative. As they needed to be consumed almost immediately after being made, fresh sausages were considered luxury items in pre-industrial Europe. In line with their short shelf life, they often contained perishable ingredients such as eggs and cream, as well as highly expensive ones such as saffron and nutmeg. A good example of a medieval style fresh sausage is the French boudin blanc (see page 22). Fresh sausages have always been the most popular kind in Britain, where cured and smoked varieties have never made much headway, possibly due to the excellence of the local ham and bacon.

The most significant developments in the world of sausages in the last 500 years have been, first, the transportation of traditional European recipes to the Americas and other former colonies and, second, the Industrial Revolution. Mechanisation has transformed the production of sausages, often to the detriment of their quality. In recent years, however, there has been something of a backlash. More and more people are making their own sausages, whether out of ethical concerns about mass production, growing culinary sophistication or both. A sausage renaissance is underway!

THE ULTIMATE SAUSAGE EXPERIENCE

Few things are as good as a good sausage but the reverse is also true. Most people have had a ghastly sausage experience, be it an undercooked banger at a barbecue or a revolting casserole at school. Unfortunately, the very nature of sausages makes it tempting for big businesses to 'bury' substandard ingredients in them. They are frequently made with poor-quality meat from animals raised in distressing conditions and the practice of bulking them up by injecting them with water has become routine. 'That's okay; it's all mashed up together so no-one will notice the difference', some commercial producers tell themselves. Anyone who has eaten top-quality sausages knows otherwise. There are essentially two ways of ensuring that's what you get. You can either buy them from reputable suppliers or you can make them yourself.

Great sausages are packages of goodness made with top-quality ingredients. In our opinion, the best examples are those in which the contrast between the outside and the inside is maximised. Nothing can beat a freshly cooked banger with a crunchy, caramelised exterior and a juicy, fragrant interior, unless it's a carefully fermented variety with a dry skin and meltingly soft contents.

TYPES OF SAUSAGE

There are various ways of classifying sausages but, for the purposes of this book, we've grouped them into the following categories:

Fresh sausages Neither cooked nor cured during the manufacturing process, fresh sausages need to be cooked and consumed within a few days of being made (alternatively, you can store them in the freezer for three to six months). They contain few preservatives other than salt, which is primarily present as a flavour enhancer. Fresh sausages are usually fried or grilled. Classic British bangers like the Cumberland (see page 16) and the Lincolnshire fall into this category, as do continental varieties such as the Toulouse (see page 17).

Precooked sausages As the name implies, sausages in this group are cooked or partially cooked as part of the making process. This is usually done either by blanching them in very hot water, as with Boudin Blanc (see page 22), or by hot smoking them, as with Polish Wiejska (see page 25). Most varieties of precooked sausages need to be heated again before they are eaten. Typical examples include Frankfurters (see page 24) and Saveloys (see pages 24–25).

Cured sausages This is the category into which the likes of Salami (see page 20) and some kinds of Chorizo (see pages 18–19) fall. They are designed to be eaten raw but also make excellent cooking ingredients. Cured sausages need to be matured over several weeks or months in a cool, fairly humid environment before they are eaten. During this period, a process of fermentation occurs. Curing is all about arranging things so that 'good' bacteria thrive while the growth of 'bad' bacteria is inhibited. The chief weapons in this battle are salt, temperature and humidity control and, sometimes, the use of starter cultures. Cured sausages are designed for keeping – in other words, they can be consumed over a period of several weeks without significant deterioration.

Skinless sausages and sausage meat Sausage mixes that would normally be filled into casings can make excellent cooking ingredients. They can be formed into patties, meatballs or dumplings or used as beautifully moist stuffings.

Sausage cousins Haggis, black pudding and the like are definitely part of the sausage family but are distinctive enough to form a clan of their own.

Fish and veggie sausages This self-explanatory category demonstrates that sausage eating is far from a no go area for non meat eaters.

HOW THE BOOK WORKS

The Sausage Book is based on the assumption that you may or may not want to make your own sausages, but you'll certainly want to make sausage-based recipes. In this chapter, we show you in detail how to make a representative sausage of each of the three main kinds (fresh, precooked and cured), followed by brief instructions on making other sausages within those families, including many that appear in our recipes. If you don't wish to make your own sausages, skip straight to the recipes. As well as showing you how to make your own sausages and some of the delicious dishes you can create with them, for inspiration we've included a number of features on superior artisan sausage makers – these are some of the best producers in the world. (Our only regret is that we couldn't make it to Italy, the home of many of the planet's finest sausages. The blame lies with the Icelandic volcano.) There is also a feature on Johnny's experience of keeping pigs – an often overlooked but important and rewarding part of the sausage-making process. We conclude with an A–Z of the world's sausages which, though far from comprehensive, we hope will further whet your appetite.

MAKING YOUR OWN SAUSAGES

You don't need to make your own sausages to enjoy our recipes but, if you do, it will increase your appreciation of them immeasurably. Sausages are among the most satisfying items to make at home. The process is great hands-on fun and the feeling of achievement that comes with producing a perfectly matured, top-quality salami or chorizo is tremendous. You never know quite what's in 'supermarket' sausages – they often contain artificial preservatives and may be bulked up with water and other tasteless fillers. They also may not have been given enough time to mature properly. If you make your own sausages, none of this need apply. And you don't have to put up with the preferences of Mr and Mrs Average. If you like your chorizo extra spicy, just make it that way.

EQUIPMENT AND HYGIENE

Hygiene is always important in food preparation and is absolutely vital when making sausages. Mincing meat greatly increases its surface area and therefore its vulnerability to bacterial infection. The consequences of this happening to fresh sausages are bad enough; with cured ones, they can be catastrophic. Keep your hands and equipment scrupulously clean. Johnny swears by Milton fluid.

As far as equipment goes, the home sausage maker needs the following:

Mincer Ideally, this would have three plate sizes: fine, medium and coarse. Some mincers double up as sausage stuffers, which saves you from having to buy one of each piece of equipment.

Sausage stuffer You fill the cylinder with sausage meat, then lower the plunger, which extrudes the mixture through a nozzle into the sausage casing. Manually operated stuffers offer more control than electric ones. Chose a robust model with no crannies in which sausage meat can lodge and fester.

Nozzles Usually made of plastic, nozzles are used to get sausage fillings into their cases. They attach to your mincer or sausage stuffer (with which they may be supplied) and are available in various gauges in line with the varying diameters of different sausage casings. We'd recommend you to buy three: a narrow one for chipolatas, a medium-sized one for average-sized sausages and a big one for salamis and chorizos.

Accurate kitchen scales Sausage-making ingredients need to be precisely weighed, especially curing salt and starter cultures. Choose a model that weighs in grams.

Casings (skins) You can choose between natural casings (made from animal intestines), artificial but animal-derived ones (made from collagen) and cellulose ones (suitable for vegetarians). The last two types are not suitable for frying. Casings are available in a range of widths. Beef casings are wider than hog ones, which are wider than sheep casings. Your choice of nozzle should reflect the casings you are using. Buy casings from good butchers or online. Some suppliers wind them around spools, which makes life easier but adds to the cost. Others tie little plastic rings around the ends to help you locate them. When using natural casings, rinse them thoroughly of salt (they are packed in it to help preserve them) and soak them in tepid water for about an hour before stuffing them.

Disposable latex gloves Wear these when handling sausage meat, for hygiene purposes.

Butcher's string Use this to tie off the ends of stuffed casings.

Sterilised pin or needle You will need this for piercing stuffed casings in order to remove air pockets inside the sausages.

If you plan on making cured sausages, you will also need:

Maturing chamber Unless you're prepared to spend a fortune, you'll have to use your ingenuity here. You need to create an environment in which the temperature is maintained at 10–15°C, and the humidity, at 70–80 per cent. You also need some air circulation. Nick uses an old fridge set to 12°C with a bucket of salt water inside to moisten the atmosphere. Johnny has a cellar with roughly the right conditions, and is able to fine-tune them by opening and closing the door and using a greenhouse heater if necessary. For more tips on making a maturing chamber, type 'Creating an Ideal Environment for Dry Curing Sausage' into a search engine and follow the links.

Hygrometer and thermometer Use the former to check that the relative humidity within the chamber is at the required level, and the latter to ensure the temperature inside the maturing chamber is within the desirable range.

Starter culture A starter culture ensures that desirable lactic-acid producing bacteria immediately get the better of their harmful relatives in a sausage mix. Buy them from www. weschenfelder.co.uk or www.sausagemaker.com.

Curing salts Curing salts can be purchased online (try sausagemaking.org) or at butcher's supply shops. They contain regular salt and sodium nitrite, which inhibits pathogenic bacteria, keeps meat from turning grey and imparts a cured flavour. Some also include sodium nitrate (saltpetre), which gradually breaks down into sodium nitrite. These substances are dangerous if ingested to excess so don't try mixing your own curing salt unless you really know what you are doing.

HOW TO MAKE
FRESH SAUSAGES

Whether you are making fresh sausages for immediate consumption or varieties such as salamis that need to be matured over several weeks, the fundamentals of the process are the same. You need to prepare your ingredients carefully, then get them safely stuffed into appropriate casings. The photographs below show how to make a simple French paysanne-style sausage, consisting of coarsely ground pork plus a few herbs.

PAYSANNE SAUSAGES

Traditional fresh sausage recipes call for salt to form two per cent of the total weight. We have reduced this to one and a half per cent, as it's healthier and doesn't adversely affect the flavour.

Makes about 20 sausages

- 1.5kg pork shoulder, cut into chunks
- 500g hard pork back fat, trimmed of all skin, cut into chunks (NB Instead of the 2 ingredients above you could use 2kg fatty pork belly, trimmed of skin and bone and cut into chunks)
- 15g fresh thyme, finely chopped
- 30g flat leaf parsley, roughly chopped
- 30g fine or flaky sea salt
- 10g freshly ground black pepper
- 20g garlic, chopped
- approx 3m length of spooled hog casings, soaked in warm water prior to usage

Before you start, make sure your surfaces and equipment are scrupulously clean. You may also want to wear latex gloves.

The process begins with grinding the meat **(1)** to the desired texture, which in this case is on the rough side (use a 5–7mm plate). Make sure you keep the meat cold throughout. This isn't just a matter of hygiene – if you allow sausage meat to warm up, it turns into unmanageable glue.

The next stage is to chop up the herbs and add them to the mince with the requisite quantity of salt **(2)**. You then mix the ingredients by hand until they are evenly distributed.

Now comes the slightly suggestive business of rolling the casing onto the nozzle. With any luck, one end of the casing will be wrapped around a telltale plastic ring. If it isn't, you just have to scrabble around until you find an end. Once you have succeeded, slip the end over the tip of the nozzle **(3)**, and gradually roll the whole casing onto it, bar a couple of inches. Then tie a knot in the projecting portion.

At this point, you need to load your sausage stuffer with the meat-and-herb-mixture **(4)**. Then screw the nozzle on and prepare to stuff. This will be much easier if you enlist the help of a friend. One of you turns the handle of the stuffer while the other controls the release of the casing **(5)**. This is done by gripping the part of it nearest to the tip of the nozzle between two fingers, varying the pressure as the meat emerges to ensure that the casing slips off at a controlled rate. The idea is to fill it thoroughly and evenly. All being well, you will end up with one very long sausage, but if the casing ruptures, perhaps due to some overzealous handle-turning, just tie a knot in it and start again.

When you run out of casings or meat, tie a knot in the back end as you did the front.

The final piece of the jigsaw is to twist the giant sausage into links **(6)**. There are various pretty ways of doing this but the simplest is to ease the meat into segments of the desired length through the casing, then twist at the gaps.

When it comes to cooking your freshly made sausages, do it slowly and thoroughly and do *not* prick the skins. If the heat isn't too high, there is little danger of the sausages bursting and you don't want them to lose their juiciness.

OTHER FRESH SAUSAGES

NICK'S CHIPOLATAS

Ideal for cocktail parties or with your Christmas turkey.

Makes about 40 sausages

- 1.5kg finely minced pork shoulder fillet
- 500g finely minced hard pork back fat
- 35g salt
- 10g freshly ground black pepper
- 20g garlic, chopped
- 15g fresh thyme, finely chopped
- 30g flat leaf parsley
- about 4m sheep casings

Make as per Paysanne Sausages on pages 14–15.

CUMIN SAUSAGES

India is a relatively sausage-free zone but these pork based sausages have a flavour redolent of the sub-continent.

Makes about 20 sausages

- 2kg roughly minced pork belly
- 25g cumin seeds, tossed in a pan over low heat for about 5 minutes until toasted
- 25g black onion seeds
- 35g salt
- 6g freshly ground black pepper
- 3g ground ginger
- 3g ground cloves
- about 2.5m hog casings

Make as per Paysanne Sausages on pages 14–15.

CUMBERLAND

This is our version of the classic sausage from the North West of England.

Makes about 15 sausages

- 1.2kg roughly minced thick belly pork
- 20g salt
- 5g freshly ground black pepper
- 2g freshly grated nutmeg
- 2g dried marjoram
- 2g dried sage
- 2m hog casings

Make as per Paysanne Sausages on pages 14–15, forming one giant coil. Don't tie off into links.

MERGUEZ

These spicy North African sausages can be made with beef but we prefer lamb-based ones.

Makes about 30 sausages

- 1.8kg lamb (use breast, neck or leg, but ensure that the fat content is about 25 per cent), minced through
- a medium plate
- 30g salt
- 6g black pepper
- 20g garlic, chopped
- 30g ground paprika (or Spanish pimenton for a smokier taste)
- 20g ground cumin
- 1g ground cloves
- 1g ground nutmeg
- about 3m sheep casings

Make as per Paysanne Sausages on pages 14–15.

TOULOUSE

The definitive fresh sausage of South West France.

Makes about 20 sausages

- 2kg roughly minced pork belly
- 30g relatively fine sea salt
- 2g freshly grated nutmeg
- 5g freshly ground black pepper
- 100ml red wine
- 20g garlic, chopped
- 20g flat leaf parsley, roughly chopped
- 4g fresh sage, chopped
- 4g fresh thyme, chopped
- 2.5m hog casings

Make as per Paysanne Sausages on pages 14–15.

VENISON SAUSAGES

These meaty, flavour packed sausages are perfect for barbecuing.

Makes about 20 sausages

- 1.5kg finely minced venison
- 500g finely minced pork back fat
- 150ml red wine
- 30g salt
- 10g garlic, chopped
- 5g black pepper
- 3g fresh rosemary, finely chopped
- 3g juniper berries, crushed
- 2.5m hog casings

Thoroughly mix the ingredients and fill the casing using the method shown on pages 14–15. Hang the sausages to dry for at least 24 hours in a cool airy place before cooking.

FRESH CHORIZO

Not to be confused with cured varieties of chorizo, these sausages must be cooked before being eaten.

Makes about 20 sausages

- 2.2kg roughly minced fatty pork belly
- 20g garlic, chopped
- 50g Pimenton de la Vera (hot, bitter-sweet, sweet or a mixture)
- 40g salt
- 2.5m hog casings

Thoroughly mix the ingredients and fill the casing using the method shown on pages 14–15. Hang the sausages to dry for at least 24 hours in a cool airy place before cooking.

HOW TO MAKE CURED SAUSAGES

In the world of chorizo the fundamental division is between 'cooking' varieties and those designed to be eaten raw. The latter need to be cured or, in other words, rendered safe. This is done by fermentation, a preserving process which serendipitously enhances flavour. Successful fermentation involves creating the right conditions for the growth of certain benign strains of bacteria which convert sugars in the meat into lactic acid. This has two beneficial effects: it helps protect the chorizo from acid-intolerant bacteria and it gives it its lip-smacking tang.

Here we show you how to make a cured, uncooked chorizo of the kind you might be served in a good Spanish tapas bar. The authenticity of this recipe is derived from the Pimenton de la Vera. This is a high-quality paprika from Spain, available from specialist suppliers.

CHORIZO
Makes 4–6 chorizo

- 2m beef middles (casings)
- 2kg very coarsely minced pork belly
- 20g chopped garlic
- 15g Pimenton de la Vera, hot
- 20g Pimenton de la Vera, bitter-sweet
- 25g Pimenton de la Vera, sweet
- 1.2g starter culture, dissolved in 50ml warm water
- 50g curing salt

Allow about two hours for making the chorizo if you're doing this for the first time. Make sure your work surface is scrupulously clean, ditto your sausage making equipment. We soak everything in Milton fluid for ten minutes. Ensure that your hands are thoroughly scrubbed and that there are washing facilities nearby. Gather the equipment you'll need, including a small bowl of warm water to soak the sausage skins in (to keep them moist), a sterilised pin or wooden kebab stick (to prick the casings), disposable latex gloves (to wear when handling the sausage mixture) and butcher's string (for tying off sausages). You'll also need a roll of kitchen paper handy (things can get a little messy).

Begin by soaking your beef middles in warm water until you are ready to use them. Then prepare your ingredients. We usually keep them separate, so that we can survey them before we pour them into the sausage mix. While you are preparing the ingredients keep the mince in the fridge. You want it to be very cold. If it isn't, it will turn uncomfortably gluey as the fat warms up. For this reason, sausage stuffing is not a hot-weather activity.

Take the mince out of the fridge and sprinkle the other ingredients on top. Make sure you scatter them well, especially the salt. Thoroughly mix using your hands **(1)**. The meat will start off loose but will become stickier and more compact after a few minutes.

Gently transfer the casing onto a large nozzle. A little water can help the process. Leave a few inches of casing hanging over the end of the nozzle and tie a knot in it. Fill the chamber with the chorizo mixture **(2)** and pack it down firmly. Pierce the end of the casing once or twice with your sterilised stick so that you don't get an air pocket appearing in your first sausage. You are now ready to go. Proceed as slowly as you like. If you become unsure at any stage, stop and evaluate the situation before you go any further.

Start turning the handle with one hand while the other gently guides the first sausage into being as it starts to appear from the nozzle.

As you start to fill the casing, bear the following in mind:
• Beef middles are very robust. Fill them thoroughly, as you want your chorizo to be nice and plump.
• Push some of the casing to the front of the nozzle from time to time to provide some slack. Keep it moist so that it slides off easily as the sausages fill.
• Give the chorizos a little prick with your wooden skewer wherever you see air bubbles appearing.
• Once you build up confidence you will be able to fill a couple of kilos into casings in a few minutes.

Once you have filled your casing **(3)** tie a knot at the end of it. Then tie off the sausages into 30cm lengths **(4)**, each with a loop at one end. Prick each sausage all over to aid the drying process **(5)**. Incubate the chorizo for 12–24 hours in a warm, very humid place (at around 90 per cent humidity) to activate the starter culture and kick-start the fermentation process **(6)** – a hot shower left to run intermittently in a clean and sealed bathroom should do the trick.

Hang the chorizo for six to eight weeks at 12–15°C at 70–80 per cent humidity (a hygrometer and thermometer are useful here, see page 13) until their weight is reduced by approximately 30 per cent. If the humidity is too low, the skins will harden, interfering with the maturing process. If it is too high, the chorizo will not dry properly and may go bad. See picture on page 2 for the finished article!

OTHER CURED SAUSAGES

KABANOS

These Polish sausages (see pictures below and opposite) make good subjects for your early curing experiments as they mature in just two weeks.

Makes about 30 sausages

- 10g caraway seeds
- 2kg pork belly, trimmed of skin, bone and cartilage and roughly minced
- 12g freshly ground black pepper
- 5g Colman's mustard powder
- 30g curing salt
- about 3m sheep casings

Toast the caraway seeds in a pan for three to four minutes, stirring continuously. Then mix the ingredients together, place them in a shallow open tray and refrigerate overnight.

The following day, mix the ingredients again, either in a bowl or a food mixer with a paddle attachment, until they are sticky. Then fill the mixture into the casings and tie the sausages into 15cm links.

Dry the kabanos in a cool, airy place for 24 hours. Cold smoke them (see pages 26–27) for six hours, then hang them for about two weeks until they are firm. Keep the temperature in the maturing room or chamber at around 12°C and the humidity at about 70 per cent.

SALAMI

There are endless variations on the basic theme. You could, for instance, substitute about half the pork shoulder for beef, as they do in Milan, or add a splash of white wine to the basic mix.

Makes 4–6 salami

- 1.8kg pork shoulder, roughly minced
- 700g roughly minced hard pork back fat
- 40g fennel seeds (optional)
- 30g garlic, chopped
- 10g cracked black pepper
- 70g curing salt
- 2m beef middles (casings)

Make as per Chorizo on pages 18–19.

ANCHO SALAMI

Anchos (dried poblano chillies) are used in Mexican cuisine. Sweet and mild, they give this salami a chorizo-like flavour.

Makes 4–6 salami

- 1.5kg finely diced or roughly minced pork shoulder fillet
- 500g finely diced pork back fat
- 30g dried ancho chillies, chopped
- 15g garlic, chopped
- 56g curing salt
- 25g ground paprika
- 2m beef middles (casings)

Mix the ingredients together while they are very cold, then place them on an open tray and leave in the refrigerator for 24 hours. Fill into the casings and mature for 6–8 weeks.

MILANO SALAMI

This Italian cured sausage is one of the best-known and best-selling salamis in the world.

Makes 4–6 salami

- 1kg finely minced pork shoulder fillet
- 500g finely minced beef or veal
- 500g finely diced hard pork back fat
- 6g ground white pepper
- 15g garlic, finely chopped
- 5g mixed dried herbs
- 100ml red wine
- 2g ground allspice
- 56g curing salt
- 2m beef middles (casings)

Mix the filling ingredients thoroughly and fill into the casings. Hang to mature for 6–8 weeks.

HOW TO MAKE PRECOOKED SAUSAGES

A precooked sausage is one that is cooked or partially cooked as an essential part of the manufacturing process, usually by immersion in very hot but not boiling water. Some of the world's most excellent sausages fall into this category, among them Frankfurters and boudin blanc.

Many precooked sausages are emulsified. This means that their contents are blended into a smooth paste in a way that ensures that the particles of meat and fat become bound up with water. This makes the resulting sausages particularly moist and juicy. To achieve the requisite smoothness the meat is typically finely minced twice.

There is no one-size-fits-all formula for making precooked sausages, but the two examples below – one emulsified, one 'regular' – will give you a good grounding in the basic principles.

BOUDIN BLANC

This French delicacy shares an etymological root with the English word 'pudding'.

Makes about 15 sausages

- 500g lean veal breast, finely minced twice
- 500g lean pork shoulder, finely minced twice
- 20g salt
- 3g ground white pepper
- 1g ground cloves
- 3g porcini powder (to make this, take dried porcini mushrooms and grind them in a coffee/spice grinder until powdery)
- 250g crème fraîche
- 4 eggs
- 30g flat leaf parsley
- 1.5m hog casings

Place the minced veal and pork in a food processor with the cutting blade inserted. Add the salt, pepper, cloves and porcini powder and pulse about six times until you have a sticky mixture.

Slowly add the crème fraîche, eggs and finally the parsley and blend for about a minute until you have a smooth paste, attractively flecked with parsley.

Chill the mixture in the fridge for 20 minutes, then fill it into hog casings. Twist into sausages that are approximately 12cm long.

Heat up a large pot of water and simmer the boudins at between 70°C and 80°C for 20 minutes. Turn off the heat and leave the sausages in the hot water for a further ten minutes, then chill them under cold running water.

At this point you can store your boudins in the fridge for up to five days, or freeze them, but you will probably be itching to try them. They can be prepared in various ways, including any of the following:

• Heat the boudins up in water (again), then squeeze the fillings out of the skins and serve with mustard.
• Fry the sausages in a little oil with their skins on.
• Remove the skins and gently fry the contents in butter.

LUXURY VEAL SAUSAGES

These simple, flavoursome sausages go down well with almost everybody and are extremely popular with Nick's kids. The crushed ice in the recipe serves two purposes: it prevents the meat overheating due to the friction of the revolving blades in the mincer and it provides the water necessary for the formation of a succulent emulsion. Keeping your ingredients and equipment cold is always important in sausage making but it is particularly vital when making this type of sausage. The meat you use should be at or slightly below freezing point, so give it a spell in the freezer before you start.

Makes about 30 sausages

- 500g veal breast, finely minced twice, at freezing point or slightly below
- 500g pork belly, finely minced twice, at freezing point or slightly below
- 220g streaky bacon, finely minced twice, at freezing point or slightly below
- 250g ice, blended into snow
- 3g ground white pepper
- 20g salt
- 4g mustard powder
- 1g ground mace
- 3m narrow sheep casings

Place the minced veal, pork belly and bacon in a large bowl. Add the rest of the ingredients and stir for approximately five minutes, by which time your arm will probably be aching. This can be avoided if you use a food mixer with a paddle attachment. Set it to medium speed and mix until you have a smooth paste.

Fill the sausage mix into the casings and twist off at 12–15cm intervals.

Heat up a large pot of water and simmer the sausages at between 70°C and 80°C for 15 minutes. Check the temperature with a thermometer – if it rises any higher, the casings may split. Turn the heat off and leave the sausages in the hot water for a further ten minutes. Then chill them under cold running water.

At this point you can store the sausages in the refrigerator for up to five days, or freeze them.

To cook the sausages, either fry them in a touch of oil or barbecue them. You could also try the recipe on page 85.

OTHER PRECOOKED SAUSAGES

FRANKFURTERS

In Germany, Frankfurters are made with pork. Americans base them on beef. This recipe gives you both options. We like our Franks thin, hence the sheep casings, but if you like them thicker, use hog's.

Makes about 25 sausages

- 1.4kg pork shoulder (ensure that the fat content is about 25 per cent); alternatively, use silverside of beef, including the surrounding fat
- 100g smoked streaky bacon
- 25g curing salt
- 300g ice, blended into snow
- 7g Coleman's mustard powder
- 10g ground paprika
- 3g ground mace
- 5g ground white pepper
- 10g garlic, finely chopped
- about 2m sheep casings

Cut the pork into strips and mince it through a fine plate together with the bacon. Place in the freezer until partially frozen, then repeat the mincing process.

Mix all the ingredients together either in a large bowl, or in a food mixer using the paddle attachment, for about five minutes until you have a smooth, sticky mass. Ensure the temperature remains close to freezing throughout.

Fill into the casings and tie off into 15–10cm links.

Dry the Frankfurters in a cool, airy place for 24 hours until the skins feel dry.

Either blanch the sausages at 75–85°C for 45 minutes or hot smoke them at 75–85°C for around one and a half hours until their core temperature has passed 70°C. For the best of both worlds, combine the two processes by hot smoking the Franks for about 45 minutes and then blanching them.

These Frankfurters can be stored in the fridge for up to a week or frozen. You can reheat them in a number of ways – simmer, fry, grill or barbecue.

WEISSWURST

This Munich speciality is one of our favourite emulsified sausages.

Makes about 20 sausages

- 1.1kg lean veal breast or lean pork shoulder
- 400g hard pork back fat
- 28g salt
- 400g ice, blended into snow
- 8g mustard powder
- 1.5g ground mace
- 50g parsley
- 40g low fat milk powder
- 5g white pepper
- 2.5m hog casings

Make as per Luxury Veal Sausages on page 23, only fill the weisswurst into hog casings. These excellent sausages should be reheated in simmering water, not fried. Squeeze the contents out of the casings before serving. They can be stored in the fridge for up to a week or frozen.

SAVELOYS

These saveloys are a million miles from the dismal items sold in many fish and chip shops. Traditionally, saveloys are preserved with curing salt, which turn the meat an attractive pink colour. We've used beetroot powder instead.

Makes about 15 sausages

- 1.5kg pork shoulder, finely minced twice
- 25g salt
- 5g white pepper
- 2g ground cardamom
- 1g ground mace
- 10g ground paprika
- 10g dried beetroot powder
- 2m hog casings

Chill the minced pork until it is close to freezing. Sprinkle the salt, white pepper, cardamom, mace, paprika and beetroot powder over the pork. Mix thoroughly, either with your fingers or using the paddle attachment in a food mixer, until the filling becomes smooth.

Fill into hog casings, then you can either hot smoke them at 75–85°C for around one and a half to two hours, until the core temperature of the sausages has passed 70°C (check with a probe by inserting it inside a sausage). Alternatively, simmer the saveloys at 80°C for 30 minutes, cooling them under cold running water when they're done. They will keep for a week in the fridge, or you can freeze them.

WIEJSKA

Wiejska is one of the best known smoked Polish sausages.

Makes about 15 sausages

- 2kg pork shoulder or belly, finely minced twice (aim for a fat content of around 25 per cent)
- 30g salt
- 3g white pepper
- 5g garlic

- 3g dried marjoram
- 10g sugar
- 300g ice, blended into snow
- 2.5m hog casings

Mix the ingredients together either in a large bowl or in a food mixer using the paddle attachment. Ensure the temperature of the mince is at or slightly below freezing when you commence. Fill the mixture into the casings. Hot smoke at 75–85°C for around one and a half to two hours, until the core temperature of the sausages has passed 70°C (check with a probe by inserting it inside a sausage). Wiejska can be stored in the fridge for up to a week or frozen.

Serve either cold and sliced or fried, depending on the weather/your mood/the recipe you are following.

KNACKWURST

This short, thick, cooked German beef sausage is similar to the rindswurst we saw being made in Frankfurt (pages 90–93).

Makes about 20 sausages

- 1.8kg silverside of beef, including surrounding fat, cut into strips and partially frozen, then finely minced twice
- 50g salt
- 2g ground mace
- 5g ground white pepper
- 5g ground coriander
- 300g ice, blended into snow
- 2.5m hog casings

Mix ingredients together either in a large bowl or in a food mixer using the paddle attachment. Ensure the temperature of the mince is at or slightly below freezing when you commence. Fill the mixture into the casings.

Either blanch at 75–85°C for 45 minutes or hot smoke at 75–85°C for around one and a half hours, until the core temperature of the sausages has passed 70°C. They can be frozen or stored in the fridge for up to a week.

HOW TO SMOKE SAUSAGES

There are two basic methods of smoking sausages (and for that matter, foods in general): cold and hot. The crucial difference is that cold smoking adds flavour and prolongs shelf life but doesn't cook the products it is applied to, whereas hot smoking does. If a smoked sausage is designed to be eaten raw, such as Hungarian salami, it has to be cold smoked by definition. Hot-smoked sausages can be eaten without any further cooking and some of them are designed to be, but most are heated up prior to consumption. Good examples include Frankfurters (see page 24), smoked Polish sausages or Wiejska (see page 25) and Rookwurst, a tasty Dutch sausage which we show you how to make on the opposite page.

Now to the practicalities. You have a choice between building your own smoker, which is satisfying and a lot of fun, or buying a commercial model. This needn't cost the earth. A Bradley smoker, for example, allows you to do both kinds of smoking with an excellent level of control. If you prefer to go down the DIY route, there are plenty of instructions on the Internet as well as literature on the subject – you could do worse than have a look at our book *Preserved*. Essentially, you need to construct a chamber for your sausages to hang in with an opening at the top to draw the smoke

up, plus a combustion chamber to produce the smoke. This will consist of a grate, onto which you place the hardwood chips or sawdust that will smoulder to provide the smoke. Never use soft woods like pine – they will taint the flavour of your sausages.

If you are cold smoking, which requires a temperature of 30°C or less, the combustion chamber needs to be some distance away from the smoking chamber so that the smoke cools down en route (you'll need to link the two chambers with aluminium tubing or similar). If hot smoking, which requires a minimum temperature of around 75°C, you can place the heat source directly under the smoking chamber. Nick uses an old cider barrel as a smoking chamber, Johnny, a galvanised metal dustbin. The final piece of equipment you need is a temperature probe. This will tell you a) the temperature inside the smoking chamber, which can be adjusted by changing the setting of your camping stove and/or by opening or closing the aperture at the top of the chamber and b) the internal temperature of the sausages, which is ultimately what matters when you are hot smoking.

SMOKED ROOKWURST

There are more kinds of hot-smoked than cold-smoked sausages, so to illustrate the smoking process we've chosen rookwurst, a heavily spiced Dutch hot-smoked sausage.

Makes about 20 sausages

- 1kg veal breast, finely minced twice, at freezing point or slightly below
- 1kg thick pork belly, finely minced twice, at freezing point or slightly below
- 30g salt
- 10g freshly ground black pepper
- 5g ground mace
- 4g ground cardamom
- 2g ground cloves
- 20g garlic, chopped
- 300g ice, blended into snow
- 2.5m hog casings

Mix the ingredients together for at least five minutes until they form a sticky mass. Fill the stuffing into hog casings and tie off into links.

Hang the rookwurst in a cool, airy place for 12 hours to dry out somewhat. If they are wet they won't take up the smoke.

To make Nick's smoker, you will need a barrel (1). The bottom should be open and you will need to make a small hole in the top. You will also need to screw some hooks into the underside of the lid, to hang the sausages from.

Place the barrel on some breeze blocks above a camping stove, on which you lay a metal plate. Pile wood chips such as oak, beech and birch on the metal plate and ignite the camping stove. You can control the heat in the smoker by varying the flame on the camping stove.

Hot smoke the rookwurst (2, 3) at 75–85°C for around one and a half hours until the core temperature of the sausages has passed 70°C. Make sure that the barrel is covered with a piece of sacking during this process so that you don't lose the heat. You can check the internal temperature with your temperature probe by inserting it into a sausage (4).

Remove the sausages from the smoker (5) and let them dry for at least 12 hours before eating them, during which time the smoky flavours will continue to permeate through them. You can keep them in the fridge for up to a week.

You can eat your rookwurst sliced and cold but we prefer them fried. They are even better if you heat them on a barbecue.

HOW TO MAKE BLOOD SAUSAGES

Blood sausages are like Marmite – you either love them or you hate them. Don't make the mistake, though, of assuming you'll hate them just because of what's in them. They have a primal depth of flavour for which there is no substitute.

The recipe opposite is for a Spanish-style blood sausage, aka morcilla, which has a highly satisfying texture on account of the rice it contains. British blood sausages, which are generically known as black puddings, incorporate oats or barley to similar effect. French blood sausages (boudin noir) are meatier affairs, usually made without grains. In addition to blood, they typically contain offal and slow-cooked meat from a pig's head, as in the terrific version we encountered on our trip to South West France (see pages 52–55).

Ideally, such sausages should be made with fresh blood but getting hold of it can be tricky. Even if you raise your own pigs, abattoirs will only save their blood for you if you provide them with suitable containers. If you manage to remember, you will have to stir the blood while it is still warm to remove the clots as they form. You may not fancy this at six o' clock on a cold morning just as you are getting over the demise of your beloved animals. The alternative is to purchase dried blood, which needs to be reconstituted by mixing it with roughly six times its weight in water. Dried blood is made up of incredibly fine particles so, unless you are happy to inhale clouds of irony powder, we'd advise you to wear a face mask of some kind. We learned this the hard way.

MORCILLA
Makes about 20 sausages

- 1 litre fresh pig's blood, or 150g dried pig's blood
- 500g hard pork back fat, chopped into small cubes
- 1kg cooked Thai black rice or paella rice (rice swells to 2.5 times its original weight so you will need 400g of dry product)
- 100g onion, peeled and finely chopped
- 10g garlic, chopped
- 5g fresh thyme, chopped
- 50g salt
- 5g freshly ground black pepper
- 10g ground pimenton or smoked paprika
- about 4m casings (either wide hog casings or beef middles; the latter will produce sausages with more interesting shapes)

Making blood sausages is a messy business so wear latex gloves and an old apron.

If you are using dried blood, you need to combine 150g of it with about 850ml water to make 1 litre of reconstituted blood **(1)**. Do this in two stages. First, add enough water to create a smooth paste, then add the rest of the water and mix with a stick blender **(2)** so the paste is evenly diluted. If you're using fresh blood, move directly to the next stage.

Add the rice and onions to the blood **(3)** and mix together, either with a large spoon or with your fingers. Then add the garlic and other seasonings and mix thoroughly **(4)**.

Fill into casings **(5)**, ensuring you tie off the ends tightly **(6)**.

Heat a large pan of water to 80°C and immerse your blood sausages in it for one hour until fully set. Keep testing the temperature of the water with a thermometer. If it rises much above 80°C, the casings will split.

If any of the morcillas float to the surface, give them a little prick with a needle to let the air that is causing the problem out.

When you remove the sausages from the poaching liquor, either let them cool naturally or place them under cold running water for ten minutes to hasten the process.

FRESH SAUSAGES

What do merguez and Toulouse sausages have in common with uncured chorizo and the great British banger? The answer is that they are all classified as fresh sausages, which means that they haven't been cured and are sold in an uncooked state. The preservatives they contain, typically salt and herbs, are there to add flavour rather than shelf life. A couple of centuries ago, fresh sausages really did have to be eaten immediately and were therefore considered luxuries. Refrigeration and freezing have extended their life spans to around five days and a few months respectively, but they are still at their best just a few hours after emerging from the stuffing machine. The recipes in this chapter, which range from filling stews such as Toulouse Sausage and Bean Cassoulet to Toad in the Hole, demonstrate the sheer versatility of fresh sausages.

KEEPING PIGS

Veal, beef, lamb and venison all have their place in the kingdom of the meat-based sausage, but apart from areas where it is banned for religious or cultural reasons, this is a realm in which pork reigns supreme. Pig meat is so central to the sausage story that frankly, we'd have felt phoney writing a book on the subject if one or other of us hadn't raised a few pigs.

Keeping pigs is a big responsibility, morally as well as legally. If raising animals with the intention of killing them before they reach adulthood doesn't make you do at least some soul searching, you probably shouldn't be doing it at all. At the same time, there would be no domesticated pigs if people didn't breed them for their meat. No-one is going to support pigs to the end of their natural life spans for fun – they live for up to 15 years, breed like rabbits and turn into half-ton monsters. If the pork they provide (and, therefore, a good proportion of the world's sausages) is to exist, someone, somewhere is going to have to kill some pigs.

If you eat meat and have the opportunity, there's a lot to be said for taking charge of the process by raising your own pigs. For one thing, there's a basic honesty involved. You will know in the most direct possible sense where your meat has come from, namely from endearing, sentient beasts. This will give you a reverence for the meat that is hard to feel for anonymous, shop-bought packages. Secondly, keeping pigs is a lot of fun. They are endlessly fascinating and very good company. Above all though, from the perspective of this book, you will end up with fantastic pork for sausages.

With all this in mind, when Johnny moved to the country, the first thing he did was purchase a pair of Oxford Sandy and Black piglets. (Despite living in Gloucestershire, he comes from adjacent county and wanted to show loyalty to the traditional pig of his native patch.) It was their successors, Boots and Albi, who provided the raw materials for many of the items featured in this book. Thanks to the generosity of his landlord, they had a nice little patch of field to destroy during their five month residence and they never quite ran out of new territory to excavate. Pigs are compulsive rootlers and, before long, Boots and Albi had unearthed what appeared to be relics of an ancient Cotswold civilisation. They also ate the charger for the electric fence when a heavy snowfall rendered it inoperative, but that's another story...

Young pigs convert their food (in this case, pig nuts supplemented by worms, slugs, grass and several apples a day) at a prodigious rate. For every 3kg Boots and Albi ate during their lives, they put on 1kg. You could almost see them growing and, because they were indulging their natural piggy behaviours, it was obvious that most of this weight gain was muscle. By the time the sad day came to load them into the trailer, they each tipped the scales at around fifteen stone (95kg). Taking them to the abattoir was inevitably painful, but it was a consolation to know that they'd enjoyed their brief lives to the full. It was even more consoling to collect several boxes of top-quality pork from the butchers a couple of days later. The orgy of sausage making could now begin...

The pig, if I am not mistaken,
Supplies us sausage, ham and bacon.
Let others say his heart is big
I call it foolish of the pig.

Ogden Nash

SAUTÉED SAUSAGES WITH SWEET POTATO, GOAT'S CHEESE & PARSLEY

SERVES 2

1 tablespoon pine nuts

4 thick fresh sausages
(e.g. boerwors)

1 tablespoon sunflower oil
(for frying the sausages)

2 orange-fleshed sweet potatoes,
peeled and roughly diced

100g crumbly goat's cheese,
crumbled

small bunch of flat leaf parsley,
roughly chopped

You can make this recipe successfully with almost any kind of fresh sausage – we'd recommend Toulouse (see page 17). We've found it especially tasty when prepared with boerwors, a meaty South African speciality best cooked on a barbecue.

Sauté the pine nuts in a pan over moderate heat for about three minutes until well toasted. Set aside.

Fry the sausages slowly in the sunflower oil until they are evenly browned, turning occasionally. This should take about 30 minutes. (Alternatively you can barbecue the sausages.)

Meanwhile, boil the sweet potatoes for about 10 minutes until cooked, and then drain.

When the sausages are done, remove them from the pan or barbecue and cut each one into a few pieces. Set aside.

Transfer the sweet potatoes to the pan you cooked the sausages in and toss them in the remaining cooking juices over moderate heat until crisped up. (If you cooked your sausages on a barbecue, just sauté the sweet potato in 1 tablespoon sunflower oil in a fresh pan.)

Now take a large bowl, throw all the ingredients in and toss together before serving.

HAM & PARSLEY SAUSAGES WITH MELTED CHEESE & LEEKS

SERVES 4

8 ham and parsley sausages
(see below)

1 tablespoon sunflower oil

2 medium leeks, washed thoroughly
and sliced

1 tablespoon butter

3 medium potatoes, sliced and
boiled for around 15 minutes until
cooked

200g mature Cheddar, grated

a slice of fresh white bread, blended
into breadcrumbs

freshly ground black pepper

The Sausages

1.5kg cooked ham, freshly carved.
(make sure about 25 per cent of it
is fat)

150g fresh white breadcrumbs, made
by blending 2 or 3 slices of fresh
bread in the food processor

2 medium onions, finely chopped

50g flat leaf parsley, chopped

a freshly grated nutmeg

5g freshly ground black pepper

2m hog casings

We've never come across anyone selling these sausages, so for the recipe that follows you'll have to make them yourself. It will be worth it though. If you're in a hurry however, you could substitute any other mildly flavoured fresh variety. You will need a medium-sized oven dish for this simple but rather indulgent recipe.

First make your sausages. Chill the ham and fat. Cut into strips and mince through a medium plate. Place the mince in a bowl, add the rest of the ingredients and mix with your fingers until sticky. Fill the mixture into hog casings, following the instructions for making fresh sausages on pages 14–15.

When you're ready to cook, preheat the oven to 200°C.

Gently fry the sausages in the oil for approximately ten minutes or until they are browned all over.

While the sausages are frying, fry the leeks in the butter over moderate heat for five minutes, stirring frequently.

Transfer the sausages, leeks and cooked potatoes to the oven dish.

Mix the Cheddar and breadcrumbs in a bowl and add a sprinkling of freshly ground black pepper.

Top the sausages with this mix, then bake in the oven for 20 minutes until golden brown. Serve immediately.

SAUSAGE POT AU FEU WITH GARDEN VEG

This creamy French-inspired stew is ideal fare for late spring or early summer, when the constituent vegetables are in season. Toulouse sausages (see page 17) work well in this dish.

━ ━ ━ ━ ━ ━ ━ ━ ━ ━ ━ ━ ━ ━ ━ ━

Gently fry the sausages in the sunflower oil for about 15 minutes, turning frequently, until golden brown.

Meanwhile, melt the butter in a large saucepan, then add the bacon, leek, shallot and fennel. Replace the lid and slowly braise for ten minutes, giving the saucepan an occasional shake.

Add the chicken stock and new potatoes. Simmer for 20 minutes until the potatoes are cooked.

Roughly slice the sausages and add them to the pan together with the peas, tarragon, tomatoes, Dijon mustard and crème frâiche.

Simmer for another couple of minutes and the Pot au Feu will be ready to serve.

SERVES 4

8 fresh sausages

1 tablespoon sunflower oil (for frying the sausages)

1 tablespoon butter

6 thick rashers smoked streaky bacon, chopped

1 medium leek, thoroughly washed and roughly sliced

2 shallots, peeled and sliced

1 fennel bulb, sliced

750ml fresh chicken stock

16 smallish new potatoes

200g petit pois or garden peas

1–2 sprigs fresh tarragon, chopped

10 cherry tomatoes, cut in half

2 teaspoons Dijon mustard

250ml crème fraîche

SAUSAGE WITH HOME-COOKED SPICY BEANS

4–8 chipolatas or Frankfurters

1 tablespoon sunflower oil

2–4 slices of bread, toasted

The Beans

500g dried haricot beans

½ teaspoon bicarbonate of soda

The Sauce

3kg fresh ripe tomatoes, chopped

100ml cider vinegar

10 cloves

4 cardamom pods

½ teaspoon ground white pepper

½ teaspoon ground mace

½ teaspoon ground allspice

¼ teaspoon ground cinnamon

2 teaspoons smoked paprika

100g sugar

4 cloves garlic, chopped

50g sun-dried tomatoes, finely chopped

The marriage of pork products and haricot beans is deservedly popular on both sides of the Atlantic. This recipe concentrates on the beans. As far as the accompanying sausages are concerned, high-quality chipolatas or Frankfurters come to mind, but use any grilled or fried variety you fancy. The sausage in the picture is an extra-long homemade chipolata (see recipe on page 16), coiled rather than twisted into links.

Soak the beans overnight in cold water.

To make the sauce, simmer the ingredients for a couple of hours until they have reduced in volume by at least a quarter.

Pass the mixture through a food mill; the result will be a delicious thickened tomato sauce. The riper the tomatoes you use, the sweeter it will be. This recipe will yield between 1.5kg and 1.8kg of sauce.

Drain the beans, transfer to a saucepan and cover with water. Add the bicarbonate of soda (which helps soften the beans), bring to the boil and simmer for around half an hour until soft.

While the beans are cooking, cook your chosen sausages in the oil, ensuring you time it so that they are cooked just as the beans are ready.

Add the beans to the sauce. If you find there are too many of them, they freeze beautifully.

Serve on toast with the sausages.

THE GINGER PIG: UK

Borough Market, next to Southwark Cathedral in South East London, is a gathering place for some of the best food producers in Britain. Naturally, in a nation in which consuming them is second nature, many stalls sell fresh pork sausages. None has a better reputation than The Ginger Pig.

What makes the company almost unique is the degree of control it has over its products. The Ginger Pig breeds its own pigs, grows their feed and converts them into superb sausages, all within the confines of a couple of farms in North Yorkshire. For Tim Wilson, the company's founder, this is just the obvious way of doing things, but in this era of commercial specialisation, it is actually very unusual. The upshot is that the company exudes integrity, as do its products.

We woke up one windy March morning in a bed and breakfast randomly chosen on the Internet and wondered if we were actually anywhere near Grange Farm. It turned out to be 50 yards away. On strolling into the production area, a beautiful mini stone barn equipped with huge maple butcher's blocks, we found a group of Yorkshiremen making a thoroughly un-British product – garlic Toulouse sausages. They did, though, add breadcrumbs to the mix, which would be anathema to most French butchers. Andrew, who had been given the job of showing us around, explained that they helped keep the sausages moist and gave them the texture the British public expects.

As the lads moved on to making Cumberland sausages, some more features of the company's production methods came to light. One of the most striking was the inclusion of leg meat in the mixes. Most sausage manufacturers stick to less expensive cuts but evidently nothing is too good for The Ginger Pig's customers. Andrew and co do, however, add fattier shoulder meat to ensure that the end products are not too dry. They aim for a fat content of around 20 per cent, which they judge entirely by eye.

Another of the firm's selling points was revealed during a poke around the farmyard. They breed their pigs the old fashioned way, without recourse to artificial insemination. To this end, a hilariously inexperienced Tamworth boar was placed in a pen with a rather more knowing Berkshire sow. Such was her exasperation that, at one stage, she clambered onto his back to show him what to do.

As this glimpse into the private lives of Tim Wilson's pigs illustrated, several rare breeds are kept on the company's farms, among them, the large-bottomed Welsh and the stocky Saddleback.

By selective cross breeding he is able to ensure that the piglets have hybrid vigour and the best qualities of both parents. The one relative constant is the presence of at least some genes from the Tamworth, an elegant, long-nosed russet creature, in honour of which the company is named. Tamworths are particularly agile and mischievous and, therefore, more high-maintenance than many other breeds, but they are charming characters and their meat is superb. They are also tough, which comes in handy when it's −15°C on the moors.

SAUSAGE & PUY LENTIL STEW

This dish would be excellent made with Toulouse sausages (see page 17) but we've given it a British twist. Cumberland sausages (see page 16), traditionally sold in unbroken coils, are peppery, herby and delicious.

━━━━━━━━━━━━━━━━━

Fry the sausage in the oil over moderate heat for ten minutes, turning occasionally, until beautifully browned. Remove from pan. Roughly slice when cool and set aside.

Fry the carrots, onions and mushrooms in the olive oil over moderate heat, turning frequently. Once browned, add the tomatoes, wine, water, stock cube and herbs. Squeeze in the soft flesh of the garlic.

Simmer for 15 minutes and then add the lentils and sausages. Gently cook for another ten minutes, season with a touch of salt and black pepper and your dinner is ready.

SERVES 6

1.2kg sausages or large ring of Cumberland sausage

2 teaspoons olive oil

4 medium carrots, peeled and sliced lengthways

8 baby onions, peeled

4 large mushrooms, roughly sliced

1 tablespoon olive oil

4 tomatoes, chopped

500ml red wine and 250ml water

1 beef stock cube

4 fresh sage leaves, 2 sprigs thyme and 1 sprig rosemary, all roughly chopped

1 garlic bulb, top sliced off, smothered in olive oil, wrapped in foil and baked in the oven at 200°C for 30 minutes (this can be done in advance)

400g precooked Puy lentils

salt and freshly ground black pepper

SAUSAGE HOTPOT WITH WORCESTERSHIRE SAUCE

400g fresh pork sausages

1 tablespoon olive oil (for frying the sausages)

1 tablespoon butter

1 medium onion, peeled and roughly diced

½ leek, washed and roughly chopped

2 garlic cloves, chopped

2 teaspoons ground paprika

1 medium red pepper, roughly diced

2 tablespoons tomato purée

250ml red wine

1–2 sprigs thyme, chopped

2 fresh bay leaves

¼ teaspoon dried sage

750ml chicken stock

3 medium potatoes, cleaned and roughly diced

1 x 400g tin chopped tomatoes

1 tablespoon Worcestershire sauce (we like Lea & Perrins)

Nick is a Northern lad at heart and this recipe shows his roots. Hotpots, such as Lancashire's classic lamb and potato version, are very popular t'other side of the Watford Gap, being warming, comforting and easy to prepare. This sausage-based example is no exception. Try a good Northern fresh pork sausage for this dish, such as a Cumberland (see page 16) or Lincolnshire sausage.

Gently grill the sausages or fry them in the olive oil for about twenty minutes until browned. Set aside to cool, then slice into discs.

Melt the butter in a large saucepan. Gently fry the onion, leek, garlic, paprika and red pepper for ten minutes or so.

Add the tomato purée, wine, thyme, bay leaves, sage, chicken stock, potatoes, tomatoes, Worcestershire sauce and sliced sausages.

Simmer for half an hour until the potatoes are cooked. Serve with crusty bread and butter.

TOAD IN THE HOLE

Depending on the quality of the sausages and the execution, this classic British dish can be depressingly stodgy or rather magnificent. Our 'toads' of choice are pork chipolatas (see page 16) wrapped in smoked streaky bacon, served with a flavoursome onion gravy made from rich chicken stock and a good glug of booze. For this recipe you need a standard-size 12-hole muffin tin (or, of course, two six-hole ones).

Preheat the oven to 200°C. Wrap each chipolata in one rasher of bacon and bake for fifteen minutes, each in an individual muffin mould.

While they are roasting, whisk the batter ingredients together in a bowl. Remove the chipolatas from the oven and immediately ladle out the batter into the muffin moulds so there is a chipolata poking out of each one. Place the moulds in the oven and bake for a further 20 minutes until the batter is puffed up and golden brown.

While all this has been going on, you will have been making the gravy. To do this, heat up the stock and red wine in one pan while frying the onion in the butter over moderate heat in another. Continue for about ten minutes until nice and soft. Stir in the flour and slowly pour in the hot stock, whisking as you go.

Add the thyme and Worcestershire sauce and simmer gently, stirring occasionally, then season to taste with salt and pepper.

Remove the toads in the hole from the oven and serve with mashed root vegetables and lashings of gravy.

SERVES 4

The Toads

12 chipolatas

12 rashers smoked streaky bacon

The Batter

100g plain flour

1 egg

300ml milk

The Gravy

300ml chicken or beef stock

250ml red wine

1 medium onion, peeled and sliced

1 tablespoon butter

2 teaspoons plain flour

2 sprigs thyme

2 teaspoons Worcestershire sauce

salt and freshly ground black pepper

PAYSANNE POACHED WITH SPINACH, POTATOES, MUSTARD & CRÈME FRAÎCHE

SERVES 2

4 robust fresh pork sausages

1 tablespoon olive oil

4 garlic cloves, sliced

2 red onions, peeled and roughly chopped

3 medium potatoes, roughly chopped

500ml chicken stock

6 fresh sage leaves, chopped

250g spinach, washed and roughly chopped

2 teaspoons French mustard

200ml crème fraîche

This creamy, flavoursome and easy-to-cook recipe works well with any robust pork sausage such as Paysanne (see page 15), Toulouse (see page 17) or any Italian cooking sausage.

Fry the sausages in olive oil in a large pan or non-stick wok over moderate heat for five minutes, turning frequently. Remove from the pan and set aside. Put into the same pan the garlic and onion and fry for five minutes or so, stirring occasionally. Add the potatoes, chicken stock and sage, bring to the boil and simmer for 20 minutes until the potatoes are soft. Add the sausages and simmer gently for another ten minutes, then add the spinach, mustard and crème fraîche. Stir over moderate heat until the leaves have wilted, whereupon your casserole is ready.

PAYSANNE SAUSAGE WITH CEPS & ROOT VEGETABLES

This tasty casserole is excellent made with paysanne sausages such as the ones we showed you how to make on page 15. The recipe is highly versatile, though. You could make an equally good version with Toulouse sausages (see page 17) or any other robust fresh variety – even Fresh Chorizo (see page 17).

Preheat the oven to 180°C.

Steep the ceps in boiling water (just enough to cover them), leave them to cool and then chop them up. Reserve the soaking water, which you will be using in the casserole.

Place all the ingredients apart from the Gruyère in a casserole dish and mix them together with a wooden spoon. Don't forget the water from the ceps. Pour this in gently as there may be a little grit at the bottom of the bowl – avoid pouring this into the casserole.

Place the lid on the dish and bake for one and a half hours.

Remove the lid and sprinkle the cheese on top. Bake for a further 15 minutes until melted and gooey.

Serve with chunky bread.

SERVES 4

10g dried porcini mushrooms (ceps)

8 paysanne sausages

100g smoked pancetta, chopped

2 carrots, peeled and chopped

2 medium onions, peeled and sliced

2 medium potatoes, sliced

4 garlic cloves, roughly chopped

6 medium mushrooms, roughly sliced

1 x 400g tin chopped tomatoes

100ml red wine

2 teaspoons Worcestershire sauce

2 sprigs thyme

2 fresh bay leaves

100g Gruyère cheese, grated

BAKED TOULOUSE SAUSAGE WITH SAUERKRAUT & APPLES

Toulouse sausages (see page 17) couldn't be more French, but they go remarkably well with Eastern European flavourings such as paprika and caraway seeds, as this recipe demonstrates. The tartness of the sauerkraut and apples cuts through the oiliness of the sausages to memorable effect.

- - - - - - - - - - - - - - - - - - - -

Preheat the oven to 200°C.

Boil the potatoes in a large pan for ten minutes, then drain off the water and add the apples. Toss the apple-and-potato mixture with the butter and honey until the butter has melted.

Transfer the apple-and-potato mix to a large oven dish along with the Toulouse sausages, sage, salt, pepper, paprika and caraway seeds. Bake for 30–35 minutes until golden brown.

Remove from the oven and immediately mix in the sauerkraut.

Serve with great big hunks of buttered bread.

SERVES 3

4 medium potatoes, cut into large chunks

3 juicy red apples (try Jonagold – they don't break up in the oven), cored and thickly sliced

1 heaped tablespoon butter

2 teaspoons honey

6 Toulouse sausages

6 fresh sage leaves, chopped

salt and freshly ground black pepper

1 teaspoon paprika

½ teaspoon caraway seeds

200g sauerkraut from a jar or tin, squeezed to remove the liquid

BARADIEU FARM: FRANCE

The Lot-et-Garonne department of South West France is a region in which everything revolves around food. Delightful days can be passed doing nothing more taxing than wondering what you will have for lunch, buying it, preparing it, sleeping it off, then repeating the process with dinner. Local delights include Agen prunes, white asparagus and, of course, sausages. To investigate the latter, we paid a visit to Baradieu Farm, home of the Chapolard family, where three brothers (Dominique, Marc and Bruno) plus two sisters-in-law (Christiane and Cécile) were preparing their wares for the following day's market at Nérac.

The first thing we learned was the difference between saucisses and saucissons. As the splendidly moustachioed Dominique explained, the former are fresh and the latter are dried. Things evidently aren't that simple though – the first saucisses we saw had the subtitle 'seches', which means dry, and they had been hanging in a stainless steel maturing cabinet for a week! They were, however, clearly different from the adjacent saucissons. These incorporated salami-style cubes of fat and were destined to spend an additional three weeks drying in an airy barn.

We progressed to the preparation area, where the family was busily turning out saucisses de Toulouse. It was fascinating to compare the way in which the Chapolards went about their business with the boys at The Ginger Pig (see page 40), not least because the sausages they were making were ostensibly the same. The most obvious differences were the work clothes (the brothers wore hooded smocks that would not have looked out of place in the Middle Ages), the absence of breadcrumbs and the age of the animals that furnished the ingredients (the French pigs are slaughtered at 12–14 months, fully twice the age of their English equivalents).

The Chapolards make their saucisses de Toulouse in two sizes: regular and chipolata. Salt and pepper are added at the rate of 14g and 2g per kilo, a formula that also applies to the delectable rustic paté made at Baradieu. Dominique was particularly proud of the machine they used to mix the ingredients for the sausages. It had a horizontal rather than vertical screw, which, he claimed, allowed more air into the mixture and therefore produced a better flavour.

The other sausage at the centre of the family's activities was boudin noir, a blood sausage that is roughly equivalent to British black pudding. Christiane explained in detail how they are made. They take a pig's head, cut it in half and place it in a giant cauldron together with the tongue, chitterlings, some chopped bacon and skin, sliced leeks and onions, a large bouquet garni and various internal organs (the liver is saved for paté). The mixture is then boiled for four hours, whereupon the bones are removed and fresh pig's blood is added at a ratio of 30 per cent of the total weight. Next, the solid ingredients are seasoned, minced and stuffed into casings. The Boudins are then simmered in the original boiling liquid for another four hours at precisely 82°C. Finally, they are washed in boiling water, hung up to dry for a bit and chilled.

We got our chance to sample the fruits of the Chapolards' labour later in the day, when Dominique and Christiane joined us for lunch. The saucisses seches struck the Brits present as rather an acquired taste but the saucisson was delightful. The pièce de resistance, though, was a boudin noir, apple and onion salad fearlessly knocked up by Nick. Monsieur was particularly taken with this dish and it made a convert of Johnny, who is a lifetime offal-phobe.

The next day we saw the Chapolards again, this time selling their sausages, patés and other pig derived goodies in Nérac's weekly market. Their stall may have been less glamorous than some of the others but it attracted the longest queue in town.

TOULOUSE SAUSAGE & BEAN CASSOULET

When we had a small chain of gourmet soup bars in London back in the late 1990s, Toulouse Sausage and Bean Cassoulet was our most popular offering bar none. Actually more of a stew than a soup, this winning combination of herby sausages, tangy sauce and floury butter beans is perfect on a chilly day. If you want to have a go at making the sausages yourself, see the recipe on page 17.

Fry the sausages gently in a little olive oil until lightly browned, then allow them to cool. Slice thickly and set aside. Reserve all the fat and juices.

Fry the carrot, celery, onion and pancetta in the olive oil over medium heat for around ten minutes until soft. Add the passata and the stock. Add the sausage and juices, beans, bay leaf and thyme. Simmer for half an hour, then season with salt and pepper to taste.

A few minutes before the end of the cooking time, preheat the grill to its highest setting.

Sprinkle the mixture with the breadcrumbs and finish off under the grill, removing when the breadcrumbs are golden brown.

SERVES 3

1kg Toulouse sausage (or other herby variety, such as paysanne)

olive oil

2 carrots, diced

2 sticks celery, diced

1 small onion, peeled and diced

50g pancetta, diced

1 tablespoon olive oil

250ml passata

500ml chicken stock

600g cooked butter beans

2 fresh bay leaves

2 sprigs thyme

salt and freshly ground black pepper

2 tablespoons fresh breadcrumbs, mixed with a little olive oil and salt

TOULOUSE SAUSAGES WITH DUCK BREAST & BUTTER BEANS

SERVES 4

4 Toulouse sausages

500g cherry tomatoes, sliced in half

8 small shallots, sliced

8 small garlic cloves, chopped

1 sprig thyme and 4 fresh sage leaves, roughly chopped

2 duck breasts, skin on, seasoned with a little salt, pepper and herbes de Provence

2 slices bread, cut into small dice

salt and freshly ground black pepper

1 teaspoon dried mixed herbs

2 tablespoons olive oil

300g large cooked butter beans

Beans bring out the best in Toulouse sausages (see page 17) and vice versa. The two ingredients are at the heart of cassoulet, the justifiably famous stew from the South West of France. In this recipe, the sausages are combined with butter beans rather than haricots, with another regional speciality, duck breast, thrown into the mix. This is a wonderful recipe for communal dipping. Ideally, you should serve it in an earthenware dish.

Preheat the oven to 200°C. Roast the Toulouse sausages in a roasting pan with the tomatoes, shallots, garlic cloves, thyme and sage for 30 minutes.

While the sausages are roasting, fry the duck breasts skin-side down in a frying pan set over very low heat for 15 minutes, then turn them over and give them ten minutes on the other side. They should be nice and pink. Don't worry if the breasts are done before the sausages – just leave them on the side until you are ready to use them.

Place the mini croutons in a bowl and toss them around with a touch of salt and pepper, a pinch of mixed herbs and a dab of olive oil. Transfer them into a small dish and roast them alongside the Toulouse sausages for the last ten minutes of their cooking time.

Five minute before the sausages and croutons are ready, heat up the butter beans with a tablespoon of olive oil in a small pan and roughly slice the duck breast.

Transfer the baked sausage mix, butter beans and duck breast into a large earthenware dish, sprinkle the croutons on top and dig in.

SAUSAGES POACHED IN RED WINE & THYME

This is essentially posh sausage and mash served with a gutsy onion gravy. You can use any fresh sausages (see pages 14–17) but we'd recommend Italian ones with fennel seeds. You'll need a large frying pan.

—————————————————————

Gently fry the sausages and onions in the olive oil for at least 20 minutes until the onions have turned gooey.

Add the red wine, thyme, tomato purée, beef stock cube or bouillon, and sugar. Give the mixture a stir and reduce over moderate heat until the volume of the wine has halved.

To make the mash, peel and slice the potatoes, boil them for 20 minutes until soft then drain. Add the butter, milk, cheese and a little salt and pepper, and roughly mash with a potato masher.

Spoon out a hearty portion of mashed potato onto a plate and serve with sausages and the rich onion gravy.

Savoy cabbage, boiled and tossed in butter, would be a perfect accompaniment for this dish.

SERVES 4

8 fresh sausages

2 medium red onions, peeled and roughly sliced

1 tablespoon olive oil

½ bottle red wine

4 sprigs thyme, chopped

1 tablespoon tomato purée

1 beef stock cube or
1 teaspoon beef bouillon

1 teaspoon sugar

The Mash

6–8 medium potatoes

1 tablespoon butter

100ml milk

100g Gruyère cheese, grated

salt and freshly ground black pepper

BASQUE SAUSAGE WITH OYSTERS

For maximum authenticity, you would make this luxurious starter with Basque chorizo, which is called *txistorra*. This can be difficult to track down, let alone pronounce. Fortunately you can substitute any fresh chorizo (see page 17).

━ ━ ━ ━ ━ ━ ━ ━ ━ ━ ━ ━ ━ ━ ━

Fry the sausages over moderate heat for ten minutes until nicely browned. Remove from the pan and set aside.

Pour away most of the oil from the frying pan and briefly fry the courgette in the same pan over moderate heat. Remove from the heat and stir in the parsley.

Slice the sausages on the diagonal into big chunks. Place a mound of courgette on each plate. Top with the chorizo and position the oysters on the side. Sprinkle with sea salt and serve.

SERVES 2

2 fresh (uncured) chorizo

2 medium courgettes, roughly grated or cut into strips

small handful of flat leaf parsley, finely chopped

4 oysters

sea salt

MERGUEZ WITH COUSCOUS

1 heaped tablespoon sesame seeds, toasted in the oven at 180°C for 5 minutes

1 teaspoon ground sumac (a tangy spice from the Middle East)

1 teaspoon dried thyme

½ teaspoon salt

8 merguez sausages

200g dry couscous

1 tablespoon olive oil

supermarket-sized bunches (25g) of flat leaf parsley and fresh mint, roughly chopped

juice of 1 lemon

2 tablespoons green olives, roughly chopped

2 tablespoons shelled pistachios, toasted in the oven at 180°C for 5 minutes

seeds from ½ fresh pomegranate

The merguez sausage (see page 17) is a spicy, red North African speciality, so good that the French, who are picky about these things, have adopted it as their own. Made with lamb, beef or a mixture of both, it is traditionally served with couscous.

Pound the toasted sesame seeds, sumac, thyme and salt in a mortar with a pestle. If you don't have a pestle and mortar, just mix these ingredients together in a small bowl, crushing them with a spoon as you go.

Fry the merguez in a medium-sized frying pan over moderate heat for 10–15 minutes, turning occasionally until cooked.

While the merguez are frying, mix the dry couscous with the olive oil and just cover with boiling water. Leave to soak for five minutes.

In a large bowl mix the couscous with the herbs, lemon juice and olives and any extra juices left over from frying the merguez.

Top the couscous with the pistachios, pomegranate seeds and spice mix. Serve with the merguez and hot flat bread.

CHORIZO BAKED WITH APPLE & RED ONION

4 apples, cored and cut into quarters

4 red onions, peeled and roughly cut into quarters

1 tablespoon olive oil

16 fresh (uncured) mini chorizo, or 8 regular sized ones

250ml cider

8 fresh sage leaves

2 sprigs rosemary

This is an odd sounding yet truly delicious combination. Try making the chorizo sausages on page 17 for this dish.

Heat the oven to 180°C.

Toss the apple and onion with the oil in a medium-sized baking dish. Add the chorizo, cider, sage and rosemary and bake for 40 minutes until the liquid has become somewhat gooey.

Serve with fresh sourdough bread.

CHORIZO WITH SQUID

The combination of chorizo and squid has become a staple in restaurants all over the world. Here is how to make it at home.

— — — — — — — — — — — —

Preheat the oven to 240°C. Bake the red pepper for 15 minutes until charred, then leave to cool. Peel off the skin and remove the seeds.

Place the flour-and-semolina mix in a freezer bag along with the squid and shake until the tubes and tentacles are thoroughly coated. Set aside.

Using a stick blender or small food-processor, purée the red pepper with the olive oil and balsamic vinegar until smooth. Set aside.

Fry the chorizo in a small frying pan over moderate heat until nicely charred on each side.

While the chorizo is frying, heat up the sunflower oil in a deep-fat fryer until shimmering hot and briefly fry the coated squid for two or three minutes until crispy.

Place a pile of rocket on each plate, top with the chorizo and squid and dress with a generous swirl of the roasted red pepper dressing.

SERVES 3

1 tablespoon semolina mixed with 1 tablespoon plain flour and 1 teaspoon dried mixed herbs

8 cleaned baby squid (available frozen or on the fish counter; they usually come with the tentacles stuffed inside – these should be used as well)

3 fresh (uncured) chorizo, cut in half lengthways

sunflower oil for deep-frying

100g rocket

The Dressing

1 large red pepper

1 tablespoon olive oil

1 tablespoon balsamic vinegar

CHORIZO PAELLA WITH SEAFOOD

This dish is scented with saffron and has a rich, smoky tomato flavour. Have a go at making the fresh chorizo shown on page 17, or even the cured version shown on pages 18–19, which can also be used for this recipe. Both have a depth of flavour that really adds savour to this dish. But shop-bought chorizo will be delicious here, too. Don't worry if you don't have a paella pan – use a large wok instead.

Fry the garlic, shallots and chorizo in the olive oil over moderate heat for at least five minutes, stirring frequently.

Add the pimenton and rice. Keep the pan on the heat and 'toast' the rice for a couple of minutes, stirring constantly so it doesn't stick.

Add half the stock, the saffron and the tomatoes and cook gently until the liquid has been taken up by the rice. Add the rest of the stock and, once it has come to the boil, add the squid and shrimp.

Simmer the rice until al dente, stir in the parsley and serve.

SERVES 4

2 garlic cloves, chopped

2 shallots or 1 medium red onion, finely chopped

2 fresh or cured chorizo (120–150g), sliced

1 tablespoon olive oil

2 teaspoons Spanish pimenton

250g paella rice

700ml chicken stock

pinch of saffron

4 tomatoes, chopped

250g baby squid (available ready cleaned from most supermarkets)

250g large raw prawns

small bunch of flat leaf parsley, roughly chopped.

HUEVOS RANCHEROS WITH CHORIZO

2 fresh (uncured) chorizo, sliced

½ onion, peeled and chopped

½ red chilli, sliced

½ red pepper, chopped

200g chopped tomatoes from a tin

1–2 sprigs oregano, chopped

salt

2 eggs

This classic Hispanic breakfast dish, which uses fresh chorizo (see page 17), will set you up for the day nicely. You will need a small to medium frying pan with a lid.

Fry the sliced sausages for a few minutes over moderate heat, then add the onion, chilli and pepper and continue to fry for five minutes or so, until the fat has been released from the chorizo. Give the mixture an occasional stir.

Add the tomatoes, oregano and a little salt if you wish. Simmer for ten minutes.

Make two indentations in the sauce and break in the eggs.

Place the lid on the pan and continue to cook over low to moderate heat for three to five minutes until the eggs are done to your liking.

Place the pan on the table and serve yourselves.

Warm corn tortillas are an essential accompaniment.

SWEET & SOUR SAUSAGES

SERVES 4

8 fresh sausages or 12 chipolatas

1 teaspoon sunflower oil (for frying the sausages)

3cm block of ginger, peeled and thinly sliced

1 red pepper and 1 green pepper, roughly diced

1 medium onion, peeled and roughly diced

10 baby corn

2 teaspoons sesame seeds

small bunch of coriander

3 tablespoons tomato ketchup

1 tablespoon sweet chilli sauce

1 tablespoon teriyaki sauce

This recipe is tailor made for Nick's Chipolatas (see page 16) and vice versa. If you want to go all-out Oriental, you could use lap cheong, but ensure you steam them first. You'll need a non-stick wok for this dish.

Fry the sausages in the sunflower oil in the wok over moderate heat for about 15 minutes until cooked, turning frequently. Remove from the pan and set aside.

Using the oil that has seeped out from the sausages, stir-fry the ginger, peppers, onion, baby corn and sesame seeds over moderate heat for five minutes until a touch charred.

Turn the heat right down and slice in the sausages, adding all the lovely juices that flow out of them when you slice them.

Finally, add the coriander, ketchup, and chilli and teriyaki sauces and simmer for about a minute.

Serve with noodles or rice.

PASTA WITH WILD BOAR SAUSAGES

Wild boar sausages are strongly flavoured and so go well with this intense tomato sauce. The slight bitterness of the radicchio complements them too.

Preheat the oven to 130°C. Season the cherry tomatoes with 1 tablespoon olive oil, add the rosemary and balsamic vinegar and roast for one and a half to two hours until sweet and sticky.

Grill the wild boar sausages or fry them in the sunflower oil over moderate heat for about 20 minutes until attractively charred. Slice when cooked and set aside.

While the sausages are frying, boil the pasta and drain.

Sauté the radicchio in 2 teaspoons olive oil over moderate heat for a few minutes, then place all the ingredients in a large bowl and toss them all together.

Serve topped with shavings of Parmesan.

SERVES 4

500g cherry tomatoes

olive oil

2 sprigs rosemary

1 tablespoon balsamic vinegar

8 fresh wild boar sausages

1 teaspoon sunflower oil (for frying the sausages)

400g dried pasta (such as conchiglie, fusilli or penne)

2 heads of radicchio, sliced

20 black olives, pitted

block of Parmesan cheese

VENISON SAUSAGE WITH HONEY-GLAZED CARROTS

SERVES 4

8 thick venison sausages

1 teaspoon sunflower oil (for frying the sausages)

600g carrots, peeled and cut into long strips

1 tablespoon butter

2 teaspoons caraway seeds

300ml cider

1 sprig thyme

1 tablespoon honey

salt and freshly ground black pepper

Venison sausages (see page 17) usually incorporate a certain amount of pork fat as the meat is otherwise too lean. They are robust in flavour and go very well with sweet, slow-cooked carrots.

Slowly pan-fry the sausages in the oil for 30 minutes or so, giving them an occasional turn.

Place the carrots in a large open pan along with the butter, caraway seeds, cider, thyme and honey, and season with a little salt and black pepper.

Cook over low to moderate heat until the cider has almost completely evaporated. There will be much stickiness at the bottom of the pan, so ensure you stir the carrots frequently – once the sauce becomes sticky there is a tendency for them to burn.

Serve with sautéed potatoes.

PRECOOKED SAUSAGES

If a sausage is cooked, semi-cooked or hot smoked (see pages 26–27) as an integral part of its manufacturing process, it falls into the precooked category. Many of the world's favourite sausages are members of this club, among them Frankfurters, boudin blanc and savalovs. Eating a hot dog made with a sausage you have created is a pleasure not to deny yourself. At the other end of the scale, this chapter includes recipes that could grace the menu of a Michelin starred restaurant, such as the sumptuous Veal Sausage with Morels in a Creamy Sauce. Understandably, some precooked sausage makers guard their secrets jealously. A couple of the recipes in this chapter are based on varieties — saucisse de Montbéliard and Morteau — that we frankly don't know how to make. If you want to try them out you'll need to buy in the relevant sausages, either from a smart deli at home or while you're on holiday in France.

WEISSWURST WITH CREAMY SPAETZLE

SERVES 4

8 weisswurst

350g dried spaetzle (egg noodles)

150g Emmenthal cheese, grated

100ml crème fraîche

2 teaspoons French or sweet mustard

scrunched up handful of flat leaf parsley, roughly chopped (optional)

salt and white pepper

Weisswurst (see page 24) are delicate, creamy, white Bavarian sausages made from veal. They sneak into this chapter because they are scalded after stuffing but don't let this fool you into thinking they have a long shelf-life – Bavarians traditionally won't eat weisswurst after noon on the day they are made. The classic way of consuming them is to suck the contents out of the casing, but you probably won't mind being spared that pleasure on this occasion. If you don't have weisswurst, you can use other smooth sausages such as Frankfurters (see page 24) or Boudin Blanc (see page 22) for this recipe instead.

Prepare two large pans of boiling water. Remove one of them from the heat and drop in the weisswurst.

Drop the spaetzle into the other pan and boil until al dente. Drain the noodles and return them to the saucepan.

Stir in the Emmenthal, crème fraîche, mustard and parsley (if using), season with salt and white pepper and dollop onto plates.

Drain the weisswurst, cut lengthways and peel off the skin. Place on top of the spaetzle and serve.

POTATO SALAD WITH GRILLED FRANKFURTERS

SERVES 4

3 medium potatoes

2 medium carrots

4 large eggs

8 Frankfurters

2 teaspoons vegetable oil

6 medium pickled gherkins,
roughly diced

2 teaspoons capers

1 sprig flat leaf parsley,
roughly chopped

2 spring onions, roughly chopped

1 tablespoon fresh dill,
roughly chopped

2 tablespoons good mayonnaise

1 teaspoon French mustard

2 tablespoons crème fraîche

salt and freshly ground black pepper

squeeze of lemon juice

This zingy salad is perfect for a summer party or any other time you have a cold beer in your hand.

Peel the potatoes and cut them into 1cm cubes. Do the same to the carrots. Boil them together for ten minutes until cooked, then rinse under cold water to cool them down. Set aside.

Hard boil the eggs for eight minutes, then peel and cut into 1cm dice.

Cut the Frankfurters lengthways, coat with a touch of vegetable oil and grill, fry or barbecue until nicely crisped up.

Place the potatoes, eggs, carrots, gherkins, capers, parsley, spring onion, dill, mayo, mustard, crème fraîche, salt, black pepper and lemon juice in a larger bowl and mix together gently. Serve with the warm Frankfurters.

FRANKFURTERS WITH PETIT POIS & MELTING CHEESE

8 Frankfurters

about 250g dried macaroni

200g cream cheese

2 tablespoon double cream

salt and white pepper

250g frozen petit pois

small block of mature
Cheddar cheese

This comfortingly gooey dish is a proven hit with both adults and kids. The petit pois add a touch of colour to what would otherwise be a rather monochrome dish. If you're keen to try making your own Frankfurters to use in this recipe, follow the instructions on page 24. Why not get the kids involved?

Grill the Frankfurters and slice them into thick chunks.

Boil the macaroni in a large saucepan until cooked, then replace in the saucepan as soon as you've drained it and add the cream cheese and cream. Stir until the cream cheese has melted, then season to taste.

Add the peas and Frankfurters, then transfer the mixture to an oven dish. Grate a generous layer of Cheddar on top and grill for about five minutes until golden brown.

VEAL SAUSAGE SCHNITZEL WITH MUSHROOM SAUCE

A coating of breadcrumbs has as positive an effect on a good veal sausage (see Luxury Veal Sausages, page 23) as it does on a beaten out escalope of the same meat.

(see Luxury Veal Sausages, page 23)

Preheat the oven to 200°C.

First make the sauce. Slice the top off the head of garlic and place the decapitated bulb on a square of foil. Season it with a little salt and pepper, drizzle with olive oil and wrap it up into a little foil parcel. Bake for 30–35 minutes until soft and squidgy, remove from the oven and leave to cool.

Fry the mushrooms in a saucepan in a big blob of butter until cooked, then add the sage and thyme. Take the garlic in your hand and squeeze the soft roast paste into the pan. Cook over moderate heat for another couple of minutes, stirring continually. Add the crème fraîche and the grated nutmeg. Stir the mixture over low heat until everything has melted together and season to taste.

Coat the sausage slices in flour. Dip them in the beaten egg and toss in the breadcrumbs until coated.

Pour enough olive oil into a frying pan to shallow-fry the sausage slices and cook them for three minutes on either side over moderate heat until golden brown. Serve with the mushroom sauce.

Sautéed potatoes make an excellent accompaniment to this dish.

SERVES 3–4

The Sausages

6–8 cooked veal sausages, roughly sliced

2 tablespoons plain flour

2 eggs, lightly beaten

4 slices fresh white bread, blended into breadcrumbs in a food-processor

olive oil for frying

The Sauce

1 garlic bulb

olive oil

salt and freshly ground black pepper

200g mushrooms, sliced

1 tablespoon unsalted butter

4 fresh sage leaves, chopped

1 heaped teaspoon thyme, chopped

200ml crème fraîche

approx ½ nutmeg, freshly grated

CURRYWURST WITH CHIPS

8 Frankfurters

The Curry Sauce

1 medium onion, peeled and diced

2 teaspoons chopped garlic

1 tablespoon chopped ginger

1 red chilli, chopped

50g butter

2 tablespoons curry powder

1 x 400g tin chopped tomatoes

1 tablespoon tomato purée

100ml crème fraîche

200ml coconut cream

The Chips

8 medium potatoes (varieties such as Maris Piper, Estima and Rooster work well), scrubbed clean but not peeled, and cut into chips

oil for deep-frying

flaky sea salt

If you want a recommendation for this dish, ask a German. Over 800 million portions of hot sausage with curry sauce are sold in Germany every year. You don't have to use Frankfurters (see page 24) – more or less any precooked German sausage will do.

To make the curry sauce, gently fry the onion, garlic, ginger and chilli in the butter for around five minutes. Add the curry powder and stir in thoroughly.

Add the tinned tomato, tomato purée, crème fraîche and coconut cream and simmer for ten minutes to allow the spices to release their flavours.

Heat the sausages in a pan of boiling water. As soon as you add the sausages to the pot, take the pan off the heat and leave it to one side until you need the sausages.

Cook up four portions of chips (or buy them from a takeaway). Gently fry them in the oil at roughly 110°C until cooked but uncoloured, then remove them from the oil. Heat the oil further until shimmering (roughly 160–180°C) and fry the chips for a further three to four minutes until golden brown. Remove from the pan and drain on kitchen paper. Season with flaky sea salt if you like.

Cut the Frankfurters into chunks, pour the curry sauce over them and serve with the chips.

BOUDIN BLANC WITH MORELS IN A CREAMY SAUCE

This is an impressive little dish for an intimate dinner party, hence the quantities given in the recipe. Serve it as a starter for two, or double the quantities to make it a main course. The morel is a reassuringly expensive dried mushroom with a unique texture and exquisite flavour. Our Boudins Blancs (see page 23) are tailor made for this dish, but you could easily substitute Luxury Veal Sausages (see page 22) or Weisswurst (see page 24).

Place the morels in a small bowl and just cover with boiling water. Leave them to soak for 30 minutes, remove from the water and set aside. Reserve the liquid – it will have absorbed delightful mushroomy flavours and you will need it later.

Gently fry the sausages in the butter very slowly for about half an hour, turning occasionally.

While the sausages are frying, make the sauce. First, slice the morels and lightly fry them in 1 tablespoon butter for five to eight minutes. Add the water you soaked the fungi in, taking care to omit any grit, plus the wine and chicken stock, and reduce rapidly until the sauce has become gelatinous. Throw in the parsley or chervil and crème fraîche, simmer for a minute or two, and the sauce is ready.

Serve the sausages with the sauce poured over, with delicate Chinese greens such as pak choi.

SERVES 2

2 boudins blancs or veal sausages

The Creamy Sauce

10 medium dried morels

knob of unsalted butter

200ml red wine

200ml chicken stock

2 heaped tablespoons crème fraîche

1 tablespoon flat leaf parsley or fresh chervil, chopped

BOUDIN BLANC WITH CRUSHED POTATOES & CARAMELISED RED ONIONS

50g butter

olive oil

500g red onions, peeled and sliced

1 tablespoon balsamic vinegar

2 small sprigs rosemary

4 small sprigs thyme

salt and freshly ground black pepper

20 new potatoes

5 garlic cloves, peeled

4 boudins blancs

100ml double cream

1 tablespoon chopped flat leaf parsley

Whether you're eating them or making them, boudins blancs are among the least threatening of all sausages. If you want to make your own, see the instructions on page 22. If you don't, you'll find these French delicacies are widely available in the shops.

Melt the butter with 50ml olive oil in a medium-sized saucepan. Add the red onions, balsamic vinegar, rosemary, and half the sprigs of thyme and seasoning. Simmer gently for 30–40 minutes until the onions are sweet and soft, stirring frequently as they cook.

Place the new potatoes in a medium-sized saucepan that has a tight-fitting lid along with 1 tablespoon olive oil, the garlic, the remaining thyme and a little seasoning. Fry very gently for 30–40 minutes – the same amount of time that it takes to cook the onions. Give the pan a vigorous shake from time to time.

Place the boudins in a small frying pan with 2 teaspoons olive oil and cook over gentle heat, turning occasionally, until golden brown.

Transfer the cooked potatoes to a bowl, add the cream and parsley and barely crush with a fork or potato masher. Serve alongside the boudins blancs, scattered with the caramelised red onions.

BRATWURST COOKED IN BEER

4 fresh bratwurst

a dash of sunflower oil

1 large onion, peeled and sliced

1 tablespoon butter

250ml tasty beer

400g spring greens, plunged into boiling water and cooked for a couple of minutes, then chilled under the cold tap

100ml double cream

½ nutmeg, freshly grated

salt and freshly ground black pepper

The bratwurst, bound together with eggs and cream, is one of Germany's sausage aristocrats. Not surprisingly, it is thoroughly at home in a beer-based sauce.

Fry the bratwurst in a saucepan in a dash of oil over low heat, turning frequently to ensure even browning. This should take around 15 minutes.

Add the onion, butter and beer. Simmer for 20 minutes or so until the beer has become syrupy and the onions are soft.

Slice the cooked spring greens and add them to the pan along with the cream, nutmeg and seasoning.

Bring to the boil, then serve immediately with hunks of crusty bread and some butter.

BRETON SAUSAGE & WHITE WINE POTÉE

A potée is essentially a wholesome pork and vegetable soup. The Breton sausage in question is Andouille de Guémené, a large smoked sausage made from chitterlings (pig's intestines). For once we admit defeat on the making front. Just buy some from a delicatessen! Alternatively, you could use andouillette or virtually any other kind of sausage.

The heart is the 'plug' at the base of an artichoke, above the stalk. All around it are petals (not good to eat), while deeper inside, directly connected to the top of the heart, is the fluffy choke (even less nice). To prepare an artichoke, ease your knife down the sides of the vegetable, trimming the green petals to their base where they are much paler in colour. Next, plunge your fingers into the centre of the artichoke and pull away the fluff and fine petals from the top of the heart. Once you have secured your prize, dice it and squeeze a touch of lemon juice over it to stop it discolouring. Set aside.

Gently fry the onion, carrot, lardons, celery and fennel in the butter for 10–15 minutes in a lidded pan, giving the contents an occasional stir. Add the artichoke, potatoes, chicken stock, white wine and herbs and simmer gently for at least 30 minutes until the vegetables are cooked.

Stir in the crème fraîche and season with a touch of salt and freshly ground black pepper.

Pan fry the slices of andouille over moderate heat until browned on each side and serve as a garnish on each portion of soup.

SERVES 4

2 fresh artichoke hearts

squeeze of lemon juice

1 onion, peeled and roughly diced

1 carrot, peeled and roughly diced

100g smoked lardons

2 sticks celery, sliced

1 fennel bulb, sliced

1 tablespoon butter

2 medium potatoes, peeled and chopped

750ml chicken stock

½ bottle white wine

2 fresh bay leaves, 2 sprigs thyme and 4 fresh sage leaves

100ml crème fraîche

salt and freshly ground black pepper

8 medium slices andouille de Guémené

GREF-VÖLSINGS: GERMANY

No book on sausages could do justice to the subject without a field trip to Germany. This is a country that boasts, at a conservative estimate, some 1,500 varieties and a per capita consumption of more than 30 kilos per year. The question was which part of this wurst-obsessed nation to visit. Candidates included Nuremberg, spiritual home of the bratwurst, and Munich, birthplace of the veal-based weisswurst. In the end, though, we plumped for Frankfurt, home of the most famous precooked sausage on earth.

Our first foray from our hotel spectacularly proved the point that Germans take their sausages seriously. It wasn't even technically lunchtime but the square adjacent to the metro station was packed with sausage-eaters. The standard offering consisted of a sausage, a generous dollop of sweet, creamy senf (mustard), a bread roll and a glass of beer or apfelwein (flat cider). Many of the crowd, though, had just the sausage with the mustard. The biggest surprise was the identity of the most popular variety. It was a thick beef offering known as the rindswurst. It isn't that the Frankfurters aren't fond of Frankfurters – they are – but they like a bit of variation. They also don't call them that unless they are selling them to tourists. Instead, the city's most famous foodstuff is known as the Wienerwurst.

To penetrate deeper into Frankfurt's sausage culture, we dropped into a traditional apfelweinlokal (cider bar) called Zum Gemalten Haus, which means the painted house. Sure enough, the outside of the building was decorated with a delightful apple-tree motif. We sat in the garden and ordered the house speciality. This consisted of a mound of sauerkraut decorated with four kinds of sausage: blut und leberwurst (blood and liver), bratwurst, two Wienerwurst and a fat rindswurst. As tradition dictates, the dish was accompanied by a bowl of tangy green sauce made from fresh herbs. There was no danger of going home empty. Dennis, our waiter, couldn't have been more obliging. He posed for photographs and acted as though a visit from a group of sausage-loving British authors was a daily event.

The following day, we had a 7am meeting at Gref-Völsings, the city's most famous sausage manufacturer, in the Hanauer Landstrasse. It was here, in 1894, that the citizens of Frankfurt were introduced to the rindswurst. It was created to cater for the city's growing Jewish population, for whom the traditional pork-based Frankfurter was a non-starter. Despite the earliness of the hour, the shop at street level was doing a roaring trade selling rindswurst to local workers with cups of beef stock for dunking purposes. Our main interest, however, was in what was going on in the basement, where the company makes approximately ten tons of sausages per week.

The core ingredients of Gref-Völsings rindswurst are beef neck and shoulder, which contain fat and lean meat in the desired proportions. After arriving in the production area via an ingenious rail system, the meat is placed in a giant mincer called The Wolf along with one head of fresh garlic per batch. After its initial grinding, the garlicky beef is transferred to a bowl cutter along with herbs

and spices. Several scoops of ground ice are added to ensure the formation of an emulsion (a suspension of fat particles in water), which is the key to the finished sausages' smooth texture. The ingredients are then cut into a fine purée with the consistency of paté. Great care is taken to prevent their temperature rising above 8°C.

The next stage is the filling of the sausages, which at this point are surprisingly white. They are then hot smoked for 45 minutes, followed by a period in a steam cooker, which ends when their internal temperature reaches 87°C. The rindswurst are then sprayed with cold water to cool them down, before being vacuum packed or sold loose from the counter upstairs. Naturally, we tucked into a few before leaving the premises. They were deliciously moist, with a perfectly balanced flavour.

Gref-Völsings also make traditional Frankfurters, which are a far cry from the limp items sold from street stalls all over the planet. They are made from pork, which is rarely the case in the USA for example, and have a resilience which makes biting into them a squeaky experience. They also have a noticeable tang of bacon, which is one of their defining ingredients.

HOTPOT OF ROOKWURST & KALE

SERVES 4

8 slices smoked bacon, chopped

2 medium onions, peeled and cut into sizeable chunks

2 tablespoons butter

400ml chicken stock

2 medium carrots, peeled and sliced

2 fresh bay leaves

4 medium potatoes, sliced

4 fresh sage leaves

4 rookwurst sausages

2 apples, cored and sliced

½ nutmeg, freshly grated

400g curly kale, shredded

½ glass full fat milk

salt and freshly ground black pepper

Rookwurst (see page 27) is a lovely sausage from the Netherlands, laced with spices and then smoked. This satisfying hotpot can be looked on as a Dutch version of bubble and squeak. In its native land it is known as *stamppot* or *hutspot*.

Fry the bacon and onions in 1 tablespoon of the butter for about ten minutes over moderate heat. Add the chicken stock, carrots, bay leaves and potatoes. Gently boil for around 20 minutes until the potatoes are cooked.

Add the sage, sausages, apple, nutmeg and kale and simmer on for about ten minutes.

Finally, add the milk and remaining tablespoon of butter and give everything a good stir. You may even want to use a potato masher to make the mixture appealingly mushy.

Season with salt and black pepper and serve. If you have Dutch guests, they may have tears in their eyes.

SAVELOY & VEGETABLE TEMPURA

120g plain flour

200ml water

100ml milk

8 fresh sage leaves

2 courgettes, sliced

8 baby corn, sliced in half lengthways

16 sugar snap peas

2–3 large saveloys, sliced

oil for deep-frying

The Dressing

100g mayonnaise

juice of 1 lemon

1 garlic clove, finely chopped

pinch of salt and a little freshly ground black pepper

20 chives, chopped

Saveloys (see pages 24–25) will be familiar to many British readers as those alarmingly red sausages sold in fish and chip shops. Often deep fried in batter, they don't have the most glamorous reputation, not least because it can be anyone's guess what's in them. Yet the saveloy has a noble history (it is ultimately descended from a Roman pig's brain sausage called the Cerebrus) and we think it deserves rehabilitation. Here it is given a contemporary Japanese treatment.

Begin by making the dressing. Weigh out the mayonnaise into a bowl, add the lemon juice, garlic, salt, black pepper and chives and whisk together. Set aside.

To make the tempura batter, mix the flour, water and milk together in a medium-sized bowl.

Heat the oil to 180°C, preferably in a wok.

Briefly dip the sage leaves in the batter and immediately transfer them to the oil. Deep fry for a couple of minutes until golden brown, then place on kitchen paper to soak up excess oil.

Repeat this process with the rest of the ingredients in small batches.

Serve the tempura with the dressing on the side.

SWISS CHARD BAKED WITH FRANKFURTERS & GRUYÈRE

There's no point pretending this is a dish designed with the dieter in mind, but it certainly hits the spot. You could always burn off a few calories by making the sausages yourself – the recipe is on page 24.

━ ━ ━ ━ ━ ━ ━ ━ ━ ━ ━ ━ ━ ━

Preheat the oven to 200°C.

Wash the Swiss chard and blanch it in boiling water for a couple of minutes, then chill under a cold tap and cut into manageable pieces.

Mix the butter and mustard with the warm potatoes, then transfer to a medium-sized oven dish with the Frankfurters, chard, potatoes, crème fraîche and most of the Gruyère.

Season with salt and pepper, mix together loosely and top with the remaining grated Gruyère.

Bake in the oven for 30 minutes until crisped, then serve immediately.

bunch of Swiss chard weighing around 500g

1 tablespoon butter

2 teaspoons French mustard

6 medium potatoes, sliced and boiled for around 20 minutes until soft

10 Frankfurters or other cooked emulsified sausages such as bratwurst

250ml crème fraîche

150g Gruyère cheese, grated

salt and freshly ground black pepper

SMOKED SAUSAGE CHOUCROUTE

This version of choucroute is made with fresh cabbage as opposed to sauerkraut. An Alsacien might not consider this dish entirely authentic, but it is easy to make and quite delicious. Use smoked sausages for this recipe – such as Frankfurters (see page 24) or Knackwurst (see page 25) – combined with a roughly minced country sausage such as Toulouse (see page 17).

Dry fry the mustard and caraway seeds in a small pan over moderate heat until the mustard seeds start to pop. Pour the seeds into a small bowl and set aside.

You will need to use a large saucepan that has a lid for this recipe. Fry the pancetta and onion in the butter quite gently for about 20 minutes until the onion is soft, then add the caraway seeds, black mustard seeds, bay leaves, cloves and juniper berries. Pour in the white wine and vinegar, add the potatoes and simmer for 20 minutes.

Add the cabbage and sausages and cook slowly with the lid on for ten minutes.

Add the crème fraîche and chopped parsley, season with salt and white pepper and simmer for a few more minutes.

Serve the choucroute with mustard, beer and rye bread.

SERVES 4

2 teaspoons black mustard seeds

2 teaspoons caraway seeds

500g smoked pancetta or smoked streaky bacon, cut into bite-sized pieces

2 red onions, peeled and thinly sliced

1 tablespoon butter

3 fresh bay leaves

6 cloves

6 juniper berries

½ bottle white wine

50ml white wine vinegar

2 medium potatoes, peeled and sliced

1 small head of Savoy or other cabbage, cored and very thinly sliced

4 smoked sausages

4 roughly minced country sausages

1 tablespoon crème fraîche

2 tablespoons parsley, freshly chopped

salt and white pepper

WIEJSKA WITH ROASTED GARLIC MASH

1 garlic bulb

2 sprigs rosemary

olive oil

4 medium to large potatoes, peeled and roughly chopped

2 red onions, peeled and sliced

4 slices smoked streaky bacon, sliced

100g baby spinach leaves or roughly chopped larger spinach leaves

1 tablespoon butter

1 teaspoon English or Polish mustard

2 teaspoons crème fraîche

salt and white pepper

12 thick slices wiejska sausage

Wiejska are popular Polish sausages that are slightly smoked and flavoured with marjoram. You can eat them raw but they are delicious lightly sautéed or barbecued. If wiejska prove elusive, make them yourself using the recipe on page 25, or try making this dish with any precooked sausages that appeal to you.

Preheat the oven to 200°C.

Chop the top off the head of garlic and scrunch it up in a piece of kitchen foil with a glug of olive oil and a sprig of rosemary. Roast in the oven for 35–40 minutes until soft.

Boil the potatoes for around 20 minutes, until soft, then drain them and set aside.

While the potatoes are cooking, slowly fry the onions, the bacon and the other sprig of rosemary in a tablespoon of olive oil.

Stir the spinach into the onions and then add the butter, boiled potatoes, mustard and crème fraîche. Squeeze in the pulp from the roasted garlic and apply a potato masher. Season to taste.

Briefly fry the wiejska in 2 teaspoons olive oil and serve with the mash.

KNACKWURST WITH FIVE SPICE

Germany meets China in this surprising but excellent concoction. Like many emulsified sausages, Knackwurst (see page 25) are usually poached prior to consumption, but not often in a spicy Oriental stock.

————————————————————

Simmer the chicken stock with the star anise, grated ginger, teriyaki sauce and knackwurst for ten minutes.

As the stock simmers, stir-fry the long-stem broccoli and red pepper for a couple of minutes over fierce heat, stirring constantly. Transfer to the spiced stock, then stir in the noodles and serve immediately.

SERVES 2

500ml chicken stock

4 whole star anise

1 tablespoon grated ginger

1 tablespoon teriyaki sauce

4 knackwurst

6 florets long-stem broccoli or other green vegetable

1 red pepper, cut into strips

250g cooked rice noodles

KIELBASA KRAKOWSKA WITH RED CABBAGE & CARAWAY

The smoked sausage in this recipe, flavoured with allspice, coriander and garlic, hails from Krakow, the city of pickles. The red cabbage gives this dish a suitably Central European character.

━━━━━━━━━━━━━━━━━━━━━━━━━━━━

Gently cook the cabbage, port, apples, caraway seeds and vinegar in a lidded saucepan for half an hour, stirring occasionally.

Slice the Krakowska and fry in the sunflower oil for a minute on each side. Stir into the cabbage, sprinkle with the dill and serve.

SERVES 2-3

1 small red cabbage

250ml port

2 rosy apples, sliced

2 teaspoons caraway seeds

2 tablespoons balsamic vinegar

250g Krakowska, peeled and thinly sliced

2 teaspoons sunflower oil

scattering of fresh dill

KIELBASA WITH PIEROGI

SERVES 4

2 tablespoons sunflower oil

1 onion, peeled and finely chopped

250g kielbasa or precooked sausages of your choice, sliced

1 sprig flat leaf parsley, chopped

The Pierogi Dough

225g plain flour

½ teaspoon salt

1 large egg

125g sour cream

50g butter

The Filling

100g Gruyère cheese, grated

1 large potato, peeled, cubed and boiled until soft

salt and white pepper

small bunch of flat leaf parsley, chopped

Kielbasa is the generic name for Polish sausages, most of which are smoked. One of the best ways to enjoy them is to grill or fry them, or simmer them in water, then serve with fried pierogi, Eastern European dumplings reminiscent of ravioli. Pierogi are semicircular and can be stuffed with a variety of fillings. The Gruyère and potato filling in this instance is satisfying in the way that only a full-on carbohydrate hit can be.

To make the filling, mix the Gruyère with the potato, salt, pepper and parsley in a small bowl until mushy.

To make the pierogi dough, mix the flour and salt together in a large bowl. Add the egg, sour cream and butter and stir in thoroughly. Turn out onto a surface lightly coated in flour and knead for a few minutes or, alternatively, pulse in the food-processor until smooth (eight good pulses should do it). Roll out thinly and cut into 6–8cm circles – you should have at least 12 circles.

Fill one half of each dough circle with the cheese mix, fold over the other half of the dough, squeeze out any air and press down the edges to seal.

Heat up a pot of boiling water and simmer the dumplings for five minutes. Remove from water when cooked and set aside.

Heat the oil in a large frying pan. Fry the onion and sausage over medium heat for five minutes. Remove from the pan with a slotted spoon, leaving the oil behind, and use this to fry the pierogi on each side until lightly browned.

Serve the pierogi mixed with the sausage and onions and a generous scattering of flat leaf parsley.

VIENNA MACARONI CHEESE

Confusingly, in Frankfurt, Frankfurters (see page 24) are known as Wieners, while in Vienna (Wien), Wieners are known as Frankfurters. Why each city should want to blame the other for the existence of these world-famous sausages is a mystery. Whatever you choose to call them, they definitely enhance a macaroni cheese.

Boil the cauliflower for three or four minutes in a large saucepan. Immediately cool under a cold tap, leaving the hot water in the pan.

Cook the macaroni in the cauliflower water until al dente, then drain it and return it to the saucepan. Add the cream cheese, Frankfurters, cauliflower, crème fraîche, salt and white pepper and stir over very low heat until the cream cheese has melted. This should take about a minute.

Preheat the grill to its highest setting.

Transfer the contents of the saucepan to an oven dish. Grate a generous layer of Cheddar cheese on top, then brown under the grill and serve.

SERVES 4

1 cauliflower, cut into bite-sized florets

300g dry macaroni

200g cream cheese

6 Frankfurters, sliced

100ml crème fraîche

salt and white pepper

mature Cheddar cheese for grating on top

SAUCISSE DE MONTBÉLIARD WITH FENNEL & MELTED CHEESE

Montbéliard is one of a number of French towns near the Swiss border with a reputation for fine smoked pork sausages. You could use other robust cooking sausages for this dish, but they need to be smoked to give it the requisite sweet-smoky flavour.

──────────────────────

Preheat the oven to 180°C.

Mix the olive oil, white wine, fennel and Montbéliard sausages together in an oven dish, then cover with a lid or foil and bake for one hour.

Remove the dish from the oven and increase the heat to 200°C.

Stir in the crème fraîche and mustard, then roughly slice the Camembert and lay it in slices on top of the fennel and sausages. Replace the dish in the oven and bake for ten minutes.

Serve with crusty bread.

SERVES 2

1 tablespoon olive oil

500ml white wine (preferably sweet)

2 medium fennel bulbs, sliced lengthways

2 Montbéliard sausages or other smoked sausages, cut in half

2 tablespoons crème fraîche

2 teaspoons Dijon mustard

150g Camembert or other similar soft cheese

STUFFED HOTDOGS

SERVES 2

1 medium sized onion, peeled
and sliced

1 tablespoon sunflower oil

3 medium sized potatoes, peeled
and diced

1 tablespoon butter

2 tablespoons milk

salt and freshly ground black pepper

4 medium size Frankfurters

2 tablespoons grated Gruyère,
Emmenthal or Cheddar

½ teaspoon ground paprika

Would you like to perk up your Frankfurters or add a little something to
your Wieners? This recipe provides a satisfying variation on the hotdog
theme and goes down very well with children, who may prefer the
milder taste of Emmenthal or Cheddar in the cheese topping.

Heat the grill to its maximum setting.

Gently fry the onion in the sunflower oil for ten minutes until soft.

Meanwhile, boil the potatoes for about ten minutes until soft. Drain and
then mash them with the butter, milk, salt and pepper.

Cut the Frankfurters lengthways so that they are splayed out. Place
them, cut side up, on a nice flat metal tray that will fit comfortably
under the grill.

Spread the mashed potato on the Frankfurters and top with the
fried onions.

Finally add a gentle scattering of grated cheese and a sparse sprinkle
of paprika.

Grill for ten minutes, transfer to plates and serve with mild mustard.

ROASTED VEGETABLES WITH GARLIC & SMOKED SAUSAGE

A fabulous recipe with any precooked smoked sausage such as Wiejska (see page 25), Kabanos or Frankfurters (see page 24). Not for the garlic-timid, this dish is best served warm with brown rice.

Heat the oven to 200°C.

Place the butternut squash, aubergine, red pepper, mushrooms, courgettes, tomatoes, sage leaves, garlic and thyme in a large oven dish or a roasting pan. Drizzle with olive oil and give the dish a little shuffle. Make sure the ingredients aren't sitting on top of each other. If they are, you need a bigger dish.

Bake for 40 minutes until the butternut squash is soft and the vegetables look enticingly caramelised.

Immediately stir in the sausages and the mascarpone. Season with a touch of salt and pepper.

SERVES 4

I small butternut squash, peeled, cored and roughly chopped

I small aubergine, roughly chopped

I red pepper, cored and roughly chopped

8 medium mushrooms

2 courgettes, roughly sliced

4 large tomatoes

8 fresh sage leaves

I garlic bulb, separated into cloves and peeled

2 sprigs thyme

75ml olive oil

250g smoked sausage, sliced

250g mascarpone

salt and freshly ground black pepper

CURED SAUSAGES

The distinctive tangy flavours of cured sausages are the result of fermentation, which is a process that must be managed with the greatest care. Properly prepared salamis and chorizos are like living organisms. Infact, they are teeming with them, in the form of benign bacteria. Tending tomaturing fermented sausages is like looking after hypersensitive babies. You'll find yourself running around doing absurd things to get the temperature and humidity right for the little blighters, like running hot showers in the middle of the night and bunging up the extractor fan with tissues. But the effort will be worth it. Your pride and delight when you taste your first carefully nurtured salami will be beyond words. Cured sausages are particularly at home in Mediterranean-style dishes and most of the recipes in this chapter have a whiff of Southern Europe about them.

SALAMI IN BRIOCHE WITH GRUYÈRE

When told that the Parisians were facing an acute bread shortage, Marie Antoinette supposedly quipped 'let them eat cake'. What she actually said was 'let them eat brioche'. It still wasn't the most tactful comment but brioche is a lot closer to bread than the mistranslation implies. Here it is used to make a savoury treat that lies somewhere between glorified French toast and an upmarket toasted sandwich. Salami, of course, is easy to get hold of, but if you'd like to try making your own, the recipe is on page 20.

Take a slice of brioche and arrange three slices of salami on top. Then take half the grated cheese and sprinkle it over the salami, followed by another slice of brioche. Now repeat the procedure with the remaining ingredients.

Lightly beat the eggs and milk together and dip the sandwiches in the mixture, turning them over to ensure they are thoroughly coated.

Gently heat a frying pan and pour in enough olive oil to lightly coat the surface. Slowly 'fry-toast' the sandwiches for seven to ten minutes on each side until the cheese inside has melted.

MAKES 2 SANDWICHES

4 slices brioche

6 slices salami

60g Gruyère cheese, finely grated

2 eggs

2 tablespoons milk

a little olive oil for frying

SALCHICHON SALAD WITH BAKED CHERRY TOMATOES

SERVES 2

The simplicity of this salad allows the quality of the salchichon to shine through. This recipe also works well with our Salami (see page 20).

The Salad

20 cherry tomatoes

olive oil

2 teaspoons balsamic vinegar

salt and freshly ground black pepper

A few crunchy lettuce leaves, roughly torn

50g salchichon, sliced as thinly as you can

1 avocado, skinned, cut into quarters and tossed in the juice of ½ lemon

¼ cucumber, sliced

20 fresh mint leaves

The Dressing

60ml olive oil

15ml balsamic vinegar

2 teaspoons Dijon mustard

1 teaspoon honey

juice of ½ lemon

salt and freshly ground black pepper

Preheat the oven to 150°C.

Arrange the tomatoes in an oven dish. Cover them with a dribble of olive oil, the balsamic vinegar and a little salt and pepper and bake them for an hour until shrivelled.

Place the ingredients for the dressing in a plastic container with a tight fitting lid and give it a good shake.

Place the lettuce leaves in a shallow bowl and top with the cherry tomatoes, salchichon slices, avocado quarters, cucumber and mint.

Dress the salad liberally and serve.

SLOW-COOKED PORK BELLY WITH RED WINE & CURED SAUSAGE

The British are slowly cottoning on to the merits of pork belly, having previously used it just for making bacon. This meltingly tender casserole should be slow cooked. Within reason (i.e. up to about eight hours), the longer you cook it, the better it will be. You will need a large oven dish for this recipe.

Heat the oven to 130°C.

Remove the skin from the pork belly by turning it upside down so that the skin is touching the chopping board and running a knife away from you carefully to part it from the meat.

Place the salami, Chianti, shallots, garlic, fennel, tomatoes and bay leaves in the oven dish and lay the belly on top.

Drizzle with a little olive oil and season with salt and pepper. Don't overdo the salt as the salami will release its own.

Cover the oven dish with a lid or kitchen foil and cook for at least four and as many as eight hours.

Remove the lid and increase the heat to 180°C. Continue cooking for 30 minutes to concentrate the flavours.

Serve with fresh seasonal vegetables and mashed potatoes.

SERVES 4

A thick chunk of pork belly weighing around 2.5kg

150g fennel salami, sliced thin and cut into strips

½ bottle Chianti

8 small shallots, peeled

6 garlic cloves, peeled

2 fennel bulbs, roughly sliced

6 tomatoes, sliced

2 fresh bay leaves

olive oil

salt and freshly ground black pepper

ARTICHOKE SALAD WITH SALAMI, WALNUTS & PARMESAN

SERVES 2

The Salad

6 baby artichokes

a squeeze of lemon juice

olive oil for frying

16 thin slices salami

12 cherry tomatoes, cut in half

½ small bag of rocket (about 50g)

30 walnut halves, toasted in the oven at 180°C for 5–8 minutes until slightly browned

The Walnut Pesto

2 tablespoons olive oil

juice of 1 lemon

the other half of your bag of rocket (about 50g)

½ the roasted walnuts (see above)

1 tablespoon grated Parmesan cheese

This crunchy, texturally rich salad is perfect for al fresco dining.

Pull the outer leaves off the artichokes and trim the stems. Cut in half lengthways and pull out the chokes (the fluffy bits in the middle). Cut into quarters and reserve in a small bowl of water, adding a squeeze of lemon to prevent discolouration.

To make the dressing, blend or chop the rocket and walnuts together until you have a mixture with a nicely granulated texture. Add the lemon juice, olive oil and Parmesan and stir in thoroughly.

Pour the olive oil into a frying pan – it needs to be 2–3cm deep. Heat the oil to around 180°C. If a wooden implement sizzles slightly when dipped in the oil, it's hot enough. Dry the artichokes on a kitchen paper, then fry them for eight to ten minutes, turning once, until crispy.

Combine the artichokes, salami, tomatoes, fresh rocket leaves and remaining roasted walnut halves in a large bowl and dress with the roasted walnut pesto.

ITALIAN SAUSAGE WITH TOMATO & SAGE SAUCE

SERVES 2

2 garlic cloves, chopped

2 shallots, sliced

100g salami, thinly sliced

2 tablespoons olive oil

250ml red wine

1 x 400g tin chopped tomatoes

½ teaspoon fennel seeds

6 fresh sage leaves, chopped

200–250g dried pasta of your choice

12 fresh sage leaves, used whole

oil for deep-frying

100ml crème fraîche

grated Parmesan cheese to serve

This is an excellent recipe for using up any salami you may have hanging around in the deeper recesses of your fridge. Serve it with your favourite pasta and plenty of Parmesan.

Gently fry the garlic, shallots and sliced salami in the olive oil for about eight to ten minutes until soft.

Add the red wine, tomatoes, fennel seeds and chopped sage leaves. Simmer for 20 minutes, stirring frequently.

While the sauce is simmering, cook the pasta and deep-fry the whole sage leaves. The oil in which you do this needs to be at around 170°C – in other words, shimmering. Fry the sage leaves for about a minute until crispy, then drain on kitchen paper.

Finally, spoon the crème fraîche into the sauce and stir in thoroughly. Serve the pasta mixed with the sauce and topped with Parmesan and the crispy sage leaves.

BORLOTTI BEANS WITH FENNEL & SALAMI

This is the kind of simple yet satisfying dish you might expect to be served in a farmhouse kitchen in Tuscany. Fennel and salami somehow seem to be made for each other.

Preheat the oven to 180°C.

Place the fennel, garlic, salami, cherry tomatoes and white wine in an oven dish. Spoon over the olive oil and bake for about 1 hour until cooked.

While the above mixture is baking, cook the borlotti beans. Place them in a large saucepan, cover them with water and add the bicarbonate of soda. Bring to the boil and cook for approximately 20 minutes until soft.

Mix the beans into the fennel bake, adding salt, pepper and the parsley.

Sprinkle with the garlic-infused breadcrumbs and an additional grind of salt and pepper, then bake for a further 20 minutes until golden brown.

SERVES 4

3 fennel bulbs, roughly sliced

4 garlic cloves, peeled and sliced

200g salami, sliced and cut into half moons

20 cherry tomatoes, halved

250ml dry white wine

2 tablespoons olive oil

250g dried borlotti beans, soaked overnight

½ teaspoon bicarbonate of soda

salt and freshly ground black pepper

small bunch of flat leaf parsley, chopped

2 slices bread, blended into breadcrumbs in a food-processor with 2 garlic cloves

SALAMI & OLIVE OIL FOUGASSE

Fougasse is essentially a visually striking French flatbread with holes in it. It is easy to make and becomes deliciously charred around the edges of the holes as it bakes. This version is given a savoury boost by the addition of chopped salami.

━━━━━━━━━━━━━━━━━━━━━━━━

You'll be making two batches of dough for this recipe, a day apart, so ensure you have enough ingredients for both batches before you start.

Place the flour, yeast and salt in a blender. Using the dough-making blade, pulse once or twice, then continue to do so as you add the olive oil and water through the feed tube. The dough will form into a ball. Place it in a bowl and leave it in the fridge overnight covered in clingfilm.

The following day, make another batch of dough in the same way and loosely fold it into the day-old dough together with the chopped salami. Place the enriched dough in a bowl covered with a damp cloth and leave it to rise for a couple of hours in a warm place such as an airing cupboard.

Preheat the oven to its maximum setting.

Turn out the dough onto your kitchen surface and sprinkle a little flour on it. Cut the dough into four equal pieces and shape each into a ball.

Sprinkle a baking tray with flour, or semolina if you have it. You'll have to bake the fougasse one at a time as they probably won't fit on the same tray.

Press out one ball of dough into a triangle. Cut a slit down the middle of the triangle without going all the way to the apex or base, then gently pull the sides apart until a leaf shape opens up in the middle of the triangle. Cut two more slits into the dough on each side of the 'leaf' and pull apart as before. You should have five leaf-shaped holes. Place on the baking tray and bake the fougasse for ten minutes until golden brown.

Repeat the process with the other three balls of dough.

MAKES 4

semolina for dusting (optional)

For Each Batch of Dough (NB you will therefore need twice the quantities specified below)

500g strong white bread flour, plus extra for dusting

10g fresh yeast

10g salt

50ml olive oil

300ml water

100g salami, chopped

SALAMI & AUBERGINE BAKE

SERVES 4

2 medium aubergines

olive oil

6 large tomatoes

2 balls mozzarella, weighing
about 125g each

150g salami, thinly sliced

mixed herbs

sea salt and freshly ground
black pepper

small block of Parmesan cheese

This gooey Italian bake combines salami with aubergine, a very tasty
pairing, and is a great dish for summer, when tomatoes and aubergines
are at their best. You will need a medium-sized roasting pan.

Preheat the oven to 200°C.

Slice each aubergine into six to eight slices. Lay them in a single layer in
a roasting pan and drizzle with olive oil. Bake for ten minutes, slicing the
tomatoes and mozzarella in the meantime.

Starting at one end of the roasting pan, lay the aubergine, tomato,
mozzarella and salami slices against each other at an angle so that they
overlap, forming what look like slightly collapsed rows of books.

When the dish is full, season with mixed herbs, freshly ground black
pepper and a touch of sea salt, and sprinkle with some grated Parmesan.
Finish off with a swirl of olive oil.

Bake for around 35 minutes until the protruding ingredients are crispy.
Serve with warm garlic bread.

MINESTRONE WITH FENNEL SALAMI

The Italians frequently add fennel seed to their salami mixes (see page 20), knowing from long experience how well the flavours combine. This hearty, flavour-packed soup is a good way to prove it to yourself. Even if you use regular salami, you'll still get a fennel hit from the bulb.

Pour about 1 tablespoon olive oil into a large saucepan and gently fry the salami, shallots, garlic, fennel and red pepper for around 1 minute until soft.

Add the chopped tomatoes, tomato purée, stock, rosemary and bay leaves. Simmer for 15 minutes. Add the beans and oregano.

While the soup is cooking, fry the croutons in 1 tablespoon olive oil over moderate heat. Keep stirring and they should be nicely toasted in about five minutes.

Serve the minestrone with the croutons on top.

SERVES 4

2 tablespoons olive oil

150g fennel salami or other salami, roughly chopped

2 medium shallots, peeled and roughly chopped

2 garlic cloves, peeled and chopped

1 fennel bulb, roughly chopped

1 red pepper, roughly chopped

1 x 400g tin chopped tomatoes

1 tablespoon tomato purée

500ml vegetable or chicken stock

1 sprig rosemary

2 fresh bay leaves

1 x 400g tin small white beans, drained

1 tablespoon chopped fresh oregano

2 slices bread, cut into small squares and seasoned with mixed herbs, salt and freshly ground black pepper

TOMATOES STUFFED WITH GREEN OLIVES, SALAMI & PARMESAN

SERVES 4

6 large tomatoes

18 green olives, pitted

250g chunk of salami, diced into small pieces

6 medium white mushrooms, diced

2 teaspoons capers

1 tablespoon chopped flat leaf parsley

1 teaspoon chopped fresh thyme

2 garlic cloves, peeled and chopped

1 tablespoon olive oil

2 tablespoons freshly grated Parmesan cheese

freshly ground black pepper

We would advise you to choose your tomatoes for this dish well. If you use flavourless ones, as are all too common in Northern climes, it won't be quite the same, so wait for summer, when the tomatoes are plump and ripe.

Preheat the oven to 180°C.

Cut the tomatoes in half and scoop out the insides with a spoon. Place on a non-stick baking tray.

In a large bowl, mix the olives, salami, diced mushrooms, capers, parsley, thyme, garlic, olive oil and Parmesan together and season with black pepper.

Spoon the mixture into the hollowed-out tomato halves and sprinkle the pine nuts on top.

Bake for 35–40 minutes until the topping is attractively browned.

Serve with steamed rice.

CHORIZO & SPINACH SOUP

Chorizo (see pages 18–19) goes well with many things and spinach is certainly one of them. Making this tasty dish is an excellent way of using up a length of dried sausage lounging around aimlessly at the back of the fridge.

Gently fry the chorizo, celery, garlic and onion in the olive oil in a saucepan for ten minutes or so. Add the pimenton and stir in thoroughly.

Add the chicken stock, potatoes and thyme. Simmer for 20 minutes, then mash with a potato masher.

Blanch the spinach in boiling water for a matter of seconds, then refresh under the cold tap. Finely chop it and add to the soup along with the crème fraîche, some salt and freshly ground black pepper.

This soup will store well in the fridge for a couple of days.

MAKES 4

150g chorizo, roughly chopped

75g celery (about 2 sticks), sliced

3 garlic cloves, peeled and chopped

1 medium onion, peeled and chopped

1 tablespoon olive oil

1 teaspoon picante pimenton (sweet smoked paprika)

500ml chicken stock

2 medium potatoes, diced

2 sprigs thyme

500g fresh spinach

1 heaped tablespoon crème fraîche

salt and freshly ground black pepper

CASA RIERA ORDEIX: SPAIN

The small city of Vic in Catalunya is a sleepy sort of place. Its biggest moment in recent times was hosting the Roller Hockey tournament that was one of the exhibition events at the 1992 Barcelona Olympics. Nevertheless, Vic is world famous for one thing: its air-dried sausages.

Since 1852, the definitive salchichon de Vic has been manufactured by Casa Riera Ordeix in the town's Plaza de los Martires (martyrs' square). When we arrived, we were convinced we had been given the wrong address. The building that purported to be the sausage factory was a town house with an elaborate sundial and a ceramic portrait of the eponymous saints on its facade. It looked like an upmarket apartment block. The marbled lobby we found ourselves in after ringing the bell would have confirmed this impression had it not been for a large wooden device that resembled a medieval torture instrument. On closer inspection, it turned out to be a Victorian sausage stuffer.

After a few minutes, we were greeted by Jordi, the firm's commercial director, who was friendliness and enthusiasm personified. He ushered us into an opulent wood-panelled boardroom, where we donned the overalls required to be worn in the production area with the portraits of four generations of the Riera Ordeix family staring down at us. We were shortly joined by a living member of the fifth, the current proprietor Joaquim Comelia Benet. He has the bearing of a man who is used to moving in high places. Apparently, whenever King Alfonso XII (1875–85) visited Vic, he made a point of popping into the factory after meeting with the local bishop. Senor Joaquim didn't look as though he'd be phased if Juan Carlos decided to revive the tradition.

The ground floor of the building is where the sausages are prepared and stuffed. Aside from an extraordinary glassed-off grotto housing a statue of the Madonna, it is as spic and span as any modern production facility. Jordi explained almost ruefully that the company had been forced to make changes to comply with EC hygiene regulations. But although the surroundings are now thoroughly 21st century, the recipe for the salchichon de Vic is exactly as it was when the factory first opened its doors. There is no place for artificial preservatives or starter cultures. Just four ingredients are used: lean pork leg, cubes of bacon fat, salt and black peppercorns. Having been mixed in the correct proportions, they are passed through a mincer and left to mature for 56–60 hours, whereupon they are stuffed into natural hog casings. It's that simple.

It is when the infant sausages are taken upstairs and back into the 19th century that the genius of Casa Riera Ordeix becomes apparent. The top four storeys of the building, which have slatted floors to allow air to circulate freely, are filled with thousands of sausages hanging on wooden racks, usually in complete darkness. The five to six months maturation process is controlled by two factors: moving the salchichon between storeys according to their condition (the top floors are warmer due to hot air rising) and the strategic opening and closing of windows, with which the factory is equipped on all four sides.

The aim is to keep humidity within the building at a minimum of 80 per cent. This effort is helped by Vic's foggy climate, which is the reason why the region has a sausage-making tradition in the first place. Nonetheless, the skill and judgement required of the firm's Master Curers are breathtaking. Everything must be done by instinct. A caretaker has to be on hand throughout the night in case the wind direction changes. If it does, he must immediately adjust the windows to ensure that the factory's internal microclimate remains undisturbed. The main perk of this low-tech approach is that the workers get the summer off. There are no air-conditioning machines to fall back on, so production ceases during the hottest months of the year.

The sausages are made without starter cultures. There is no need for them after a century and a half – the desired microorganisms are part of the building's fabric. As a consequence, flavour-enhancing moulds proliferate on the surfaces of the salchichon. They grow at such a rate that they have to be brushed off once a week – quite a task for one man with a tiny hand brush.

The sausages that emerge from this extended period of loving care resemble chorizos without the paprika. They have neat seams along the middle, betraying the fact that their skins are made by hand stitching two hog casings together. Anyone familiar with the slipperiness of natural casings will appreciate how difficult this must be to do, but barring the unthinkable (abandoning tradition by using other casings), there is no other way to produce salchichon with the required diameter.

The flavour of a finished salchichon de Vic has the depth and roundness of a top-notch salami, but with a firmer texture. The locals tend to cut the sausages into slices about 5mm thick and serve them on bread rubbed with chopped tomato and drizzled with olive oil. They are so good that they need no further adornment. If you are lucky enough to get hold of the genuine article, keep it in a cool, airy place, but not in the refrigerator, or you may disrupt the balance of the internal micro-flora. Salut! as they say in Catalunya.

CHORIZO & GOAT'S CHEESE TART

Goat's cheese goes particularly well with chorizo. You can roll out the pastry, make the filling and bake this tart in less than an hour. Use a shallow, non-stick pizza pan with a 1cm lip, approximately 1cm deep and 28cm across.

First make the pastry. Sieve the flour onto your kitchen work surface. Cut the butter into pieces and place on top of the flour along with the cheese, salt and nutmeg. Rub the ingredients together with the tips of your fingers until all the lumps of butter and cheese have melted into the mix. This will take a few minutes.

Make a well in the centre of the mix and fill it with the two yolks and the egg white. Work the egg in with your fingers, then gather the pastry into a ball and work it with the heel of your hand for 30 seconds. Use the pastry itself to mop up any loose bits of dough that adhere to your work surface. Work the pastry again for a minute, then shape into a ball, wrap in clingfilm and store in the fridge until you need it (you can make the pastry the day before you cook the tart).

When ready to make the tart, roll out the pastry to the approximate size of the pizza pan, lay it over it and press it down into the pan. Don't worry about trimming it around the sides unless you feel the need strongly.

Preheat the oven to 240°C. Bake the red pepper for 15 minutes until charred, then leave it to cool. Peel the skin away, remove the seeds and slice the pepper into thin strips. Reduce the oven temperature to 200°C.

Mix the crème fraîche, egg, thyme and seasoning together with a fork or whisk. Spread the mixture onto the pastry, making sure it goes all the way to the sides. Sprinkle the goat's cheese evenly on top, then lay over the roasted pepper strips in a haphazard manner, followed by the chorizo. Powder the surface with pimenton and bake for 15–20 minutes until the chorizo is nice and browned. Eat while still warm.

SERVES 3

The Pastry (enough for 1 tart)

120g plain flour

60g butter

25g grated Parmesan cheese

pinch of salt

a little grating of nutmeg

2 egg yolks from large eggs

½ the white from a large egg

The Filling

1 large red pepper

120g crème fraîche

1 large egg with 1 extra yolk

2 teaspoons chopped fresh thyme

salt and freshly ground black pepper

150g goat's cheese, crumbled

200g fresh or cured chorizo, sliced or diced

¼ teaspoon ground pimeton or any other good-quality paprika, smoked or unsmoked (according to taste)

TORTILLA WITH SALCHICHON

SERVES 4

100g salchichon de Vic or other cured sausage, thinly sliced, then cut into narrow matchsticks

4 tablespoons olive oil

400g small potatoes, thinly sliced

2 medium red onions, sliced

4 garlic cloves, peeled and each sliced into 2–3 pieces

5 large eggs, lightly beaten

small bunch of flat leaf parsley, chopped

salt and freshly ground black pepper

100g Manchego cheese, grated

1 teaspoon pimenton

This tortilla uses the bold flavour of salchichon de Vic. If you don't have any, feel free to use salami or any other cured sausage. You will need a large non-stick frying pan with a lid to cover it while the potatoes cook.

Fry the salchichon in one tablespoon of the olive oil over moderate heat for three or four minutes, then remove from the pan with a slotted spoon and set aside.

Add the remaining olive oil, the potatoes, red onion and garlic and gently fry with the lid on for 20 minutes, giving the pan an occasional vigorous shake.

Preheat the grill to its highest setting.

Add the eggs, salchichon, parsley, salt and a little ground black pepper to the potatoes and onions and stir them into the mixture.

Sprinkle the Manchego and pimenton on top and grill for five minutes until golden brown.

Serve with crusty bread and Rioja.

STIR-FRIED CHINESE SAUSAGES

Lap cheong need to be steamed prior to use as an ingredient. This is a quick and easy dish, best served with rice. You will need a wok and a steamer, although you can improvise the latter with a metal rack or colander set over a pan of boiling water.

Dry-roast the sesame seeds in a wok over moderate heat for a couple of minutes until toasted.

Steam the lap cheong for 3 minutes and then roughly slice them.

Stir-fry the ginger, spring onions, greens and Chinese sausages in the vegetable oil over quite a fierce heat for three or four minutes, tossing your wok continually.

Turn off the heat and add the sesame oil and soy sauce.

Transfer to a dish and sprinkle with the toasted sesame seeds. Serve with steamed rice.

SERVES 2

2 teaspoons sesame seeds

4 lap cheong (Chinese sausages)

4cm block of ginger, finely grated

5 spring onions, peeled and sliced

3 heads of pak choi, choi sum or other Chinese greens (or cabbage or spinach), sliced

1 tablespoon vegetable oil

1 tablespoon sesame oil

a shake of soy sauce

SESAME STEW WITH CHINESE SAUSAGES

SERVES 4

1 tablespoon sesame seeds

8 lap cheong (Chinese sausages)

sunflower oil

20 enoki, shiitake or other Oriental mushrooms

3 heads of pak choi, sliced

750ml chicken stock

4cm block of ginger, grated

5 spring onions, sliced

1 tablespoon oyster sauce

400g cooked rice noodles

1 tablespoon soy sauce

sesame oil

Nick's wife is funny about food. She declares herself wheat and dairy free but adores cream cakes. She is also a vegetarian sausage hater who loves lap cheong. She says that this dish reminds her of her childhood in Guangzhao, where her family would purchase similar stews from a street hawker at a busy crossroads.

Toast the sesame seeds in a dry pan over moderate heat for a couple of minutes until golden brown. Set aside.

Gently fry the Chinese sausages in 1 teaspoon sunflower oil, turning occasionally, until nicely browned. Set aside. (You may want to slice them before serving.)

While the sausages are frying, stir-fry the mushrooms and pak choi in 1 tablespoon sunflower oil in a wok for three to five minutes, tossing frequently.

Add the chicken stock, ginger, spring onions, oyster sauce, cooked rice noodles, soy sauce and a good glug of sesame oil. Bring to the boil and serve immediately with the Chinese sausages and sesame seeds.

SKINLESS SAUSAGES & SAUSAGE MEAT

You don't always have to go through the rigmarole of filling ingredients into casings to enjoy the flavours and textures associated with sausages. One of our favourite parts of the process of making them is frying a little patty of sausage meat before we commit to stuffing it into skins, to test the seasoning. The real point of a sausage, after all, is the mixture it is stuffed with. The qualities that make a good sausage filling – judicious seasoning, toothsome balance between fat and lean meat and so on – frequently make it an excellent cooking ingredient in its own right. Sausage meat makes an excellent stuffing for roasts, as we hope this chapter proves. It is also the basis for classic snacks such as Scotch eggs and sausage rolls, which haven't been anywhere near animal intestines.

HERBY SAUSAGE DUMPLINGS IN ROOT VEGETABLE STEW

This warming stew is very versatile — you can make the sausage dumplings with any meat you fancy, though ideally it should have a little fat in it.

Mix the dumpling ingredients together in a large bowl for a few minutes, then form the mixture into about 12 golf-ball sized dumplings.

Heat up a non-stick frying pan and fry the dumplings in the olive oil over moderate heat for a couple of minutes on each side until browned. Take off the heat and reserve in the pan with all the juices.

To make the stew, slowly fry the onion, carrot and celery in the butter with the lid on the saucepan, stirring occasionally.

Add the chicken stock, potatoes, parsnip and swede and simmer for about 30 minutes until the vegetables are cooked.

Add the leeks and dumplings with their juices and simmer for ten more minutes.

Stir in the cream and parsley and serve in large bowls.

SERVES 4

The Dumplings

500g minced pork, lamb or beef

2 small shallots, finely chopped

2–3 sprigs thyme, chopped

4 fresh sage leaves and 2 large sprigs flat leaf parsley, finely chopped

5g salt and 3g black pepper

½ a nutmeg, grated

2 teaspoons olive oil (for frying the dumplings)

The Stew

1 onion and 1 large carrot, peeled and roughly chopped

2 sticks celery, sliced

1 tablespoon butter

750ml chicken stock

2 medium potatoes, diced

2 parsnip, sliced

½ small swede, diced

1 medium leek, sliced

100ml double cream or crème fraîche

handful of flat leaf parsley, chopped

SAUSAGE PASTIES

MAKES 8 PASTIES

1 egg, lightly beaten

The Filling

12 robust fresh sausages

2 teaspoons vegetable oil

1 tablespoon olive oil

50g smoked pancetta, diced

30g unsalted butter

1 medium carrot, peeled and diced

2 medium shallots, peeled and diced

½ fennel bulb, diced

1 tablespoon plain flour

200ml chicken stock

250ml red wine

salt and freshly ground black pepper

The Pastry

250g plain flour

½ teaspoon salt

75g butter

75g suet

cold water

The pasty was invented by Cornish tin miners who didn't want to contaminate their lunches with arsenic, which was present in high levels in the mines. They held their pasties by the pastry 'crimps' which were discarded once they had eaten the rest of the packages. Pasties are traditionally filled with a mixture of beef, potato and onion. Had the good folk of Cornwall tried stuffing them with top-quality sausages, the story might have been different.

Fry the sausages in the vegetable oil in large pan over low heat for 15 minutes then remove them from the pan. When they are cool enough to handle, slice them up and set aside. Pour the olive oil into the pan, add the pancetta, butter, carrot, shallots and fennel and fry gently for eight to ten minutes. Spoon in the flour and mix it in until you can't see it anymore. Pour in a little of the stock and stir it in. The mixture will become thick and gluey. Add a bit more stock, stir it in and then pour in the rest along with the red wine and the sliced sausages. Simmer for 15 minutes, add salt and pepper if you like and leave to cool.

To make the pastry, sift the flour into a large bowl and add the salt. Add the butter and suet and rub them into the flour using the tips of your fingers. Slowly pour cold water into the bowl, squeezing and manipulating the flour-and-butter mixture as you do so, until you have a stiff dough. Turn it out onto the work surface and knead with the heel of your hand for a minute or two. Roll the dough into a ball, cover it with clingfilm and store in the refrigerator until needed.

When you're ready to make the pasties, preheat the oven to 200°C. Roll the dough into a long sausage and divide it into eight sections. Then roll each section into a ball. Take one of your balls of dough and roll it into a disc about 15cm in diameter. Place 80–100g of sausage filling in the centre of the disc and paint whipped egg around its perimeter. Then pull up the sides of the pastry and press the seams together to form a neat, pasty shaped package. Repeat the procedure seven times, then paint the outside of the pasties with the remaining whipped egg and bake them on a greased baking sheet or silicone sheet for ten minutes. At this point, reduce the oven temperature to 180°C and continue to bake for 25–30 minutes until golden brown.

SAUSAGE CANNELLONI

The Cannelloni

250g durum wheat flour ('semolato di grano duro')

2 large eggs weighing 140g in total

800g sausage meat

The Sauce

500ml milk

1 medium leek, sliced

1 small red onion, peeled and sliced

40g butter

25g plain flour

100ml crème fraîche

100g Cheddar cheese, grated

salt and freshly ground black pepper

The Topping

50g Cheddar cheese, grated

These succulent tubes of sausage meat will taste best if you make your own sheets of pasta but you can always buy some in – if so you will need about 16 sheets of fresh pasta. You can use any sausage meat you like for the stuffing – we'd recommend the mixture used to make fresh paysanne on page 15.

If you want to make the pasta yourself, place the flour in a pile on your kitchen work surface and make a well in the middle. Break the eggs into this well. Whisk them gently, gradually adding more flour from the rim of the well until all the egg is incorporated. Work the mixture with your fingers into a sticky mass and continue until it becomes smooth. It is important that you use up all the flour. Check to see whether the dough is of the right consistency. Stick your thumb in. If it comes out clean, the dough is ready. Knead the dough with the heel of your hand, half turning it as you go (always in the same direction). Knead for at least five minutes. Divide into three parts and follow the instructions on your pasta machine or roll out the dough thinly.

Your sheets of pasta (home-made or bought-in) should be about 10–12cm long. You can then cut them into widths of about 8cm.

To make the sauce, slowly heat the milk up in a pan, making sure it doesn't come to the boil.

In the meantime, gently fry the leeks and onion in the butter for ten minutes until soft, then stir in the flour. Slowly add the hot milk, stirring as you go. Add the crème fraîche and Cheddar, and season to taste. Simmer for five minutes, stirring frequently. Then take off the heat and cover the sauce with a sheet of greaseproof paper, so that a skin doesn't form. Set aside until you've prepared the cannelloni.

To do this, roll up approximately 50g of sausage meat in each rectangle of pasta.

Preheat the oven to 180°C.

Pour a little of the sauce into an oven dish and lay a single layer of cannelloni on top. Pour on some more sauce, add the rest of the cannelloni and cover with the remaining sauce.

Sprinkle the grated Cheddar on top and bake for 20 minutes. Now ramp up the heat to 220°C and continue cooking for five minutes. Serve with a pile of cooked spinach and some chunky bread.

CORN DOGS

600g fine pork mince

6g salt

2g ground white pepper

1g ground mace (1–2 pinches)

4g Colman's mustard powder

1 slice of fresh processed
white bread, blended into fine
breadcrumbs in a food-processor

1 tablespoon dried mixed herbs

200g polenta

oil for deep-frying

Corn dogs are a staple in America. Like many fast-food items, they are not always made of the finest ingredients – a typical example is a big glob of mechanically recovered sausage meat surrounded by fat-infused crispy batter – but even dodgy street corn dogs can taste fantastic, especially when dipped in ketchup. This is a healthier version with a crunchy polenta crust. You will need a 4–6cm round cutter and some wooden kebab sticks.

Place the mince in a large bowl. Add the salt, pepper, mace, mustard powder and white breadcrumbs. Mix with your fingers until you have a big gloopy mass.

Mix the herbs with the polenta and sprinkle a light layer onto your kitchen work surface.

Place the meat patty onto this layer and flatten it into a sheet approximately 1cm thick.

Sprinkle with as much polenta as will stick and then cut out your shapes. Before you remove your cutter, cut around the edges with a knife so that you're not left with unsightly strands of meat.

Thread the shapes onto kebab sticks.

Heat the oil in a wok to the point at which a wooden kebab stick fizzles when inserted into it, then fry the corn dogs for three to four minutes until thoroughly crispy.

Serve with lashings of tomato ketchup.

CHORIZO DOG

SERVES 1

1 fresh chorizo

½ red pepper, deseeded

1 length of crusty baguette

This recipe is ideal for cooking on the barbecue or frying on a griddle pan. At Borough market, our friends Brindisa serve similar 'dogs' in crusty bread with Piquillo peppers. The queues are endless.

First you will need to butterfly the chorizo: cut them down the middle lengthways and splay them face down.

Cook the chorizo and red pepper for about five minutes on each side. If you are using a barbecue, place the pepper over the hottest area and the chorizo over a somewhat cooler patch. Watch it doesn't catch fire – the fat has a tendency to ignite!

While the chorizo and pepper are cooking, slice the baguette in half lengthways and warm it either towards the side of the barbecue or under a grill.

Place the chorizo and pepper inside the bread and tuck in.

CHORIZO RAVIOLI WITH PARSLEY SAUCE

If you've never made your own pasta before, you could do much worse than start with these ravioli, which are served in a zesty parsley sauce. Just bear in mind that it is important that you get the quantities right. Full instructions are given below but, if you lack time or energy, you can always buy sheets of fresh pasta from the supermarket.

To make the pasta, place the flour in a pile on your kitchen work surface and make a well in the middle. Break the eggs into this well. Whisk them gently, gradually adding more flour from the rim of the well until all the egg is incorporated. Work with your fingers into a sticky mass and continue until it becomes smooth. It is important that you use up all the flour. Check to see whether the dough is of the right consistency. Stick your thumb in. If it comes out clean, the dough is ready. Knead the dough with the heel of your hand, half turning it as you go (always in the same direction). Knead for at least five minutes. Divide into three parts and follow the instructions on your pasta machine or roll out thinly.

Mix together the ingredients for the chorizo filling in a bowl until firm and sticky. Set aside.

Take a round cutter that's about 5–6cm in diameter and cut the pasta dough into 40 discs. This will furnish you with 20 ravioli, five for each diner. Thoroughly egg wash 20 of the pasta discs and place a heaped teaspoon of chorizo filling in the middle of each one. Cover with an un-egged disc and press down from the middle outwards to remove any air pockets. Then seal the edges of the discs by pressing them together with a fingertip.

Bring a large pan of water to the boil, simmer the ravioli for five minutes, then drain and dress with a touch of olive oil. While the ravioli are cooking, melt the butter in a small frying pan over moderate heat until it stops bubbling and starts to turn amber. Pour in the lemon juice, making the butter fizz up. Add the pepper and parsley and immediately pour over the drained and dressed ravioli. Season with a little salt and freshly ground black pepper, and serve.

SERVES 4

1 egg, lightly beaten

olive oil

salt and freshly ground black pepper

The Pasta

250g durum wheat flour ('semolato di grano duro')

2 large eggs weighing 140g in total

The Filling

250g pork belly, minced

40g freshly blended white breadcrumbs

10g ground Pimenton de la Vera

2 garlic cloves, peeled and chopped

4g salt

The Sauce

50g unsalted butter

juice of 1 lemon

freshly ground black pepper

50g flat leaf parsley, chopped

SAUSAGE ROLLS WITH ONION CONFIT

The Filling

600g finely minced pork belly or shoulder (the mince needs to about 20 per cent fat otherwise it will taste too dry)

10g salt

small sprig flat leaf parsley, chopped

6 fresh sage leaves, chopped

3 sprigs thyme chopped

1 teaspoon cracked black pepper

3 garlic cloves, peeled and chopped

The Rolls

confit of onion or onion chutney (available at most supermarkets)

tomato ketchup

250g puff pastry, thinly rolled out and cut into 8–10cm squares

These sausage rolls are easy to make and have a tempting balance of sweet and savoury flavours.

Mix the filling ingredients in a large bowl until sticky and glutinous.

On each square of pastry place half a teaspoon of onion confit, a chipolata-sized blob of sausage-meat filling and a small squiggle of ketchup. Form into a reasonably tight cylindrical roll, squeezing the edges of the pastry together. Cut two diagonal slashes on the top of the roll, then repeat the procedure until you have used up all the ingredients.

Preheat the oven to 180°C.

Bake the rolls for 20 minutes until golden brown. Serve with lashings of tomato ketchup.

SCOTCH EGGS

600g pork, finely minced (coarsely minced meat won't hold together)

50g finely blended fresh breadcrumbs

200g coarsely blended breadcrumbs, made from fresh bread with a good texture

8g salt

3g freshly ground black pepper

1g ground mace

1g ground cardamom

6 boiled eggs (boil them from cold; once up to temperature, boil for 7 minutes, then refresh under the cold tap and peel)

plain flour

1 egg, beaten

oil for deep-frying

If ever a food needed rehabilitation, it is the once not-so-humble Scotch egg. Invented by Fortnum & Mason in 1738, it has become horribly degraded in the form of cheap mass produced versions, but by making your own you can help restore this picnic delicacy to its former glory. We fry our Scotch eggs in a large wok.

Mix the minced pork, 50g finely blended breadcrumbs, salt, pepper, mace and cardamom together in a large bowl. If you have latex gloves (a must for sausage making enthusiasts), don a pair and do it with your fingers. Divide the mixture into six balls.

Coat a peeled egg in flour. Flatten a ball of sausage meat and carefully squeeze it around the egg.

Roll the ball in flour, then dip it into the whipped egg and finally roll it in the coarsely blended breadcrumbs.

Repeat this process with the rest of the eggs.

Heat the oil to 160°C in a wok and fry the Scotch eggs for eight to ten minutes until golden brown.

Serve with mustard mayonnaise or piccalilli.

ROASTED GOOSE WITH VEAL STUFFING

100g streaky bacon, chopped

1kg minced veal

250g peeled sweet chestnuts, chopped (either prepare them yourself by grilling them for 10 minutes or use ready prepared cooked whole chestnuts)

10 fresh sage leaves, chopped

150g roughly chopped onion

100g fresh breadcrumbs

excess fat from the goose (see below), chopped

1 teaspoon ground mace

generous grating of nutmeg

small bunch of flat leaf parsley, chopped

3 sprigs thyme, chopped

fine or flaky salt and freshly ground black pepper

1 large goose weighing 4.5–5.5kg (including giblets), trimmed of excess fat (which should be used in the stuffing)

½ bottle red wine

For this luxurious recipe you will need a goose weighing around 5kg (including the giblets), trimmed of any excess fat. Don't throw it away though – you will need it for the stuffing.

Preheat the oven to 180°C.

To make the stuffing, mix together in a large bowl the bacon, veal, chestnuts, sage, onion, breadcrumbs, excess fat from the goose, mace, nutmeg, parsley, thyme, 1 teaspoon of fine or flaky salt and lots of black pepper. Stuff the goose with the filling, lightly pushing it into the body cavity.

Rub the bird with salt and pepper, then place it in a roasting pan and roast it for two and a half hours.

Remove the goose from the oven and place it on a chopping board. Allow the bird to rest for at least 20 minutes before you touch it.

While the goose is resting, make the gravy. There will be a good deal of excess fat from the goose left in the roasting pan. Pour this off, then pour the wine into the roasting pan and place it on your stove top. Gently heat until the wine boils. Reduce by half, stirring and scraping as you go to dissolve all the flavoursome encrustations.

This recipe cries out for braised red cabbage, roast potatoes and apple or gooseberry sauce as accompaniments.

ROLLED PORK LOIN WITH RUSTIC SAUSAGE STUFFING

For this stunning recipe you need to use what is known as pork middle. This consists of the belly and loin together in one piece. Ask your butcher for a boned section weighing about 2kg and get him to score the skin for you. You will need some butcher's string and a roasting pan with a rack.

- - - - - - - - - - - - - - - - - -

Mix the ingredients for the stuffing together in a large bowl. Store the stuffing in the refrigerator until ready to use.

Lay the pork middle flat on a large plate or tray skin-side up and cover in a thin layer of salt. Rub the salt deep into the cracks and leave for two hours. At the end of this period, wash the salt off thoroughly and pat the meat dry.

Preheat the oven to 240°C.

Turn the meat over so the skin side is on the kitchen surface.

Mould the stuffing into a thick sausage and press it into the nook between the 'eye' of the loin (the bit that would form the meaty oval if it was used to make back bacon) and the belly section.

Roll the meat up tightly and tie with string in at least four places. Place the knots at the bottom where the extremities of the pork middle overlap.

Pour a little olive oil into a bowl and add the dried sage and dried rosemary. Season with salt and pepper and rub the mixture over the outside of the pork roll with your fingers.

Place the roll on a rack over a roasting pan – this will ensure that it crisps up nicely all over – and roast for 20 minutes, then reduce the heat to 180°C and continue roasting for an hour and 40 minutes. Serve with roast potatoes and braised cabbage.

The Roast

2kg pork middle

fine sea salt and freshly ground black pepper

olive oil

1 teaspoon dried sage

1 teaspoon dried rosemary

The Stuffing

2 sprigs thyme, chopped

10 fresh sage leaves

small bunch of flat leaf parsley, chopped

4 garlic cloves, peeled and chopped

2 teaspoons hot paprika

1 teaspoon fennel seeds

2 teaspoons coarsely ground black pepper

100ml red wine

1kg roughly minced fatty pork

SAUSAGE COUSINS

Not everything that is stuffed into an animal casing is best described as a sausage. Haggis falls into this category, as do crepinettes and faggots. Blood puddings certainly look like sausages but are sufficiently different from orthodox varieties to squeeze into this chapter. They also illustrate the point that cousins of the sausage tend not to be for the faint hearted. Blood, sheep's lungs and the like are not everyone's cup of tea. We hope, however, that the recipes that follow will tempt you to set aside any preconceptions. Some of the most prominent 'sausage cousins' depend on ingredients and techniques beyond the scope of the average home sausage maker. We're not about to teach you how to make andouillettes, for example, but we can certainly show you some good things to do with them.

BLACK PUDDING WITH CAULIFLOWER, TOPPED WITH ROASTED HAZELNUTS

This recipe is suitable for any kind of black pudding, including continental varieties such as morcilla or boudin noir. You can also make a good version with haggis. Whatever kind of sausage you use, you will end up with a dish that was easy to throw together but looks most attractive.

SERVES 4

3 tablespoons hazelnuts

1 large cauliflower

400g black pudding, crumbled or sliced

300ml crème fraîche

100g Parmesan cheese

4 sprigs rosemary

Preheat the oven to 180°C. Roast the hazelnuts for six minutes, then roughly chop them or give them a couple of seconds in the blender. Set aside. Leave the oven on.

Meanwhile, break the cauliflower into florets and blanch them in boiling water for a couple of minutes. Drain and pour into an oven dish.

Add the black pud, mix in the crème fraîche, then grate the Parmesan over the top.

Stick the sprigs of rosemary deep into the cauliflower/black pudding mixture and sprinkle with the chopped hazelnuts.

Bake in the oven for 30 minutes until golden brown and serve.

CRISPY ANDOUILLE WITH 5-SPICE

15 thin slices of andouille

½ teaspoon 5-spice

1 teaspoon teriyaki sauce

vegetable oil for deep frying

sweet chilli sauce

The andouille de Guémené, from the Loire Valley is a strange looking sausage; each slice is a visual feast of tightly packed, ever decreasing concentric circles. Made from chitterlings, the construction of this sausage is an art form. Many years ago, the *Confrerie de Chevaliers du Goutte-andouille* was formed as the guardian of this artisan process. Sadly, the society has now been disbanded after the death of its revered master. Never tell a Frenchman that you are going to fry your andouille. He'll murder you! Once they are fried they look like golden, whirling gnome's hats, at least if you are feeling sufficiently whimsical.

Coat the andouille in the spice and teryaki sauce.

Heat the oil to around 170°C. Fry the andouille for a couple of minutes until golden brown, then place on a sheet of kitchen paper to soak up the excess oil. Serve with the sweet chilli sauce.

WARM SALAD WITH SAUTÉ POTATOES & BLACK PUDDING

Black pudding has an ambiguous reputation in Britain. On the one hand, it is a staple of transport cafés, greasy spoons and the like, places not always renowned for their culinary excellence. On the other, it is increasingly popular in high-class restaurants, where its versatility is much appreciated (it goes particularly well with seafood and roast meats). This dish would be more at home in the latter than the former. It works equally well with English-style black pudding, French boudin noir and Spanish morcilla (although morcilla tends to break up in the pan).

Make the dressing in a medium sized bowl. Add the garlic and vinegar to the egg yolk and briefly whisk. Pour in the olive oil very, very slowly, whisking as you go, to create a thick dressing. Finish off with a squirt of lemon and a pinch of salt.

Cut the potatoes into cubes, boil them for ten minutes and drain. Then fry them in a large pan in olive oil over moderate heat for ten minutes until nicely browned. Set aside.

Remove the potatoes and pour off any excess oil. Fry the pancetta and black pudding for a couple of minutes on each side.

Toss the pancetta, black pudding, potatoes and watercress together in a large bowl. Decorate the salad with blobs of glistening dressing and serve.

SERVES 2

2–3 medium potatoes, unpeeled

2 tablespoons olive oil

4 thin slices smoked pancetta

6 slices of black pudding, boudin noir or morcilla

bunch of washed watercress (weighing approx 75–100g)

The Dressing

1 garlic clove, peeled and finely chopped

2 teaspoons sherry vinegar

1 egg yolk

100ml olive oil

a squeeze of lemon juice

salt

MCSWEEN: SCOTLAND

The dish that Rabbie Burns described as 'chieftain of the pudding race' is a subject of fascination for the rest of the world. It isn't just theoretical either – thanks to the effort of the marketing industry, Burns Night (January 25), on which haggis is ritually consumed along with excessive quantities of whisky, has become a fixture way beyond the boundaries of Scotland. Whether you live in Sydney or Tokyo, there is a fair chance that this delicacy will make it to your plate sooner or later. You might as well know how it's made.

To find out the answer, we travelled to the Edinburgh suburb of Loanhead, home of McSween, the world's biggest manufacturer of naturally cased haggis. The walk from the bus stop to the factory was bracing in the extreme – this was Scotland in February after all, and the hills on the horizon were sprinkled with snow – but we soon warmed up once inside the state-of-the-art facility. We were met by Jo McSween (the 'haggis queen'), a granddaughter of the company's founders, who runs the business together with her brother James. Jo is a feisty, quick-witted lady. When we had the temerity to point out that she didn't have much of a Scottish accent, she immediately responded that she toned it down so her English customers could understand her.

Traditionally, as Jo explained, the basis of a haggis was the 'pluck' of a sheep – in other words, the lungs, heart, liver and spleen. McSween, however, only use the lungs, or lites as they are known in Scotland. The other organs are considered too iron-ish and pungent. Another advantage of sticking to the lungs is the light, airy quality they give to the finished 'chieftains'. This is no great surprise when you consider their job in the living sheep. Jo showed us a huge container of raw lites. They had a pleasantly fresh aroma and definitely came from sheep who were non-smokers. Only the lobes are used – the tracheas are discarded.

The one drawback with lites is that they contain zero fat. This would make the haggises unpalatably chewy, so they are mixed with beef suet obtained from what Jo described as cows' love handles. The other key ingredients are two grades of oatmeal (pinhead and medium), which give the end products their distinctive texture, kibbled onion, which is preferred to the fresh version as there are less contamination issues, and a secret blend of spices. Jo was too smart to divulge the formula but she did admit that ground coriander seed and black pepper were among the components.

Back in the old days, the haggis mixture would be stuffed into sheep's stomachs, but this tradition has now lapsed. This is partly because the skills involved in preparing stomachs for this purpose have been forgotten and partly because a haggis made this way would weigh at least 3kg, which is impractical, given the reduced size of contemporary households. McSween now use beef bungs, which are made from the widest part of a cow's large intestine. They have to be bought in from South America and need to be soaked for two days to remove the salt in which they are packed. Each bung is slightly different in shape, which gives a pleasing variety to the finished haggises.

As we walked through the factory, we saw the various processes involved in haggis making in action. First, the lites and fat are boiled for a couple of hours and passed twice through a mincer. Next, the oats, onions and seasonings are added to the mixture, which is then stuffed into the beef bungs. These are sealed with aluminium clips, leaving little 'ears' of unstuffed casing which make the young haggises look like living creatures. The chieftains are then steam-cooked for an hour (a procedure that invariably produces a few casualties, whose skins burst as their contents expand), cooled and blast chilled. Finally, the ears are removed with a knife and the haggises are vacuum packed, which gives them a five-week shelf life.

On our departure, we were each presented with a haggis, a vegetarian version and a pack of microwavable haggis slices, a new line about which Jo is very excited. We had worked up quite an appetite by now so we headed into Edinburgh for lunch at the Whiski Bar in the Royal Mile. Naturally we ordered the 'haggis tower', made with puddings from McSween's. It took the form of a mound of buttered mashed potato and swede (neeps) with a haggis dome in a sea of thick, whisky infused gravy. It was a highly savoury dish with a lovely range of textures which quickly dispelled any lingering Sassenach anxiety about eating haggis.

A final word of warning: if you make or buy a haggis, don't be tempted to eat the casing. It should be discarded as soon as you have released the steaming contents.

HAGGIS, NEEPS & TATTIES

This is a slightly updated version of the classic Burns Night supper. Traditionally minded Scots might baulk at the crème fraîche and parsley in the vegetables but we think they improve the time-honoured formula.

Cover the haggis with kitchen foil, place it in a saucepan, cover with water, put the lid on and simmer for 40 minutes.

Meanwhile, cook the swede and potatoes in separate saucepans for around 30 minutes until cooked and drain.

For the neeps, mash the swede with the butter, crème fraîche, milk, salt and white pepper.

For the tatties, mash the potatoes with the butter, crème fraîche, milk, parsley, salt and white pepper.

Break open the haggis and serve everything together, preferably in a thick whisky enriched gravy.

SERVES 2-3

1 x 500g haggis

The Neeps

1 swede, peeled and roughly chopped

2 tablespoons butter

50ml crème fraîche

50ml milk

salt and white pepper

The Tatties

5 medium potatoes, peeled and roughly chopped

2 tablespoons butter

50ml crème fraîche

50ml milk

small sprig flat leaf parsley, chopped

salt and white pepper

CREPINETTES WITH SPINACH & ROASTED ALMONDS

SERVES 4

1 medium butternut squash, peeled, deseeded and roughly sliced

1 tablespoon olive oil

salt and freshly ground black pepper

50g flaked almonds

500g caul fat, softened in tepid water for about 1 hour

½ quantity sausage meat from Nick's Chipolatas recipe (see page 16)

400g baby spinach leaves

Crepinettes are parcels of sausage meat wrapped in caul fat, a delicate, lacy membrane that surrounds a mammal's internal organs. Caul fat comes in thin sheets and can be bought from traditional butchers.

Preheat the oven to 200°C. Toss the squash in the olive oil, salt and pepper in a roasting pan. Bake for 35 minutes until soft and browned. Put the almonds in an oven dish and pop them into the oven for the last five minutes of the cooking time. Set aside.

Peel off thin layers of caul fat and cut into eight 10cm squares. Place 100g sausage meat in the centre of each square and wrap into a neat parcel, trimming off excess fat. Shape each parcel into a thick burger shape and fry in a large non-stick frying pan or flat-bottomed wok over moderate heat for six to eight minutes on each side. Add the squash, stir in the spinach and, once it wilts, transfer everything to warmed plates. Garnish with flaked almonds. Serve with hot crusty bread.

FAGGOT & ROOT VEGETABLE STEW

SERVES 3

The Faggots

500g caul fat

600g finely minced pork belly or shoulder

10g salt

small sprig parsley, 6 fresh sage leaves and 3 sprigs thyme, chopped

1 teaspoon cracked black pepper

3 garlic cloves, peeled and chopped

The Stew

3 medium leeks, roughly chopped

6 slices streaky bacon, sliced

1 medium onion, peeled and sliced

50g butter

150ml white wine

300ml chicken stock

4 medium potatoes, thinly sliced

4 fresh sage leaves, chopped

½ nutmeg, grated

100ml crème fraîche

salt and freshly ground black pepper

Faggots are essentially British crepinettes (see page 172) – both are made by wrapping minced meat in caul fat (available from traditional butchers). Known colloquially as 'ducks' in their native English Midlands, faggots are often made with liver, hearts and other internal organs. This version omits the offal, resulting in a lighter, less metallic flavour. You will need pork belly or shoulder for this. ideally with a fat content of around 20–25 per cent.

Before you start, soften the caul fat in tepid water for an hour or so.

To make the faggots, mix the minced pork belly or shoulder with the salt, herbs, pepper and garlic in a large bowl.

Peel off thin layers of caul fat and cut into six 10cm squares. Place 100g of sausage meat in the centre of each square and wrap it up into a parcel. Trim away any excess fat. Shape each parcel into a ball.

Fry the faggots over moderate heat in a large frying pan for six to eight minutes on each side. Set aside.

Gently fry the leeks, bacon and onion in the butter in a large saucepan for 20 minutes, stirring frequently.

Add the wine, chicken stock, potatoes, chopped sage leaves and grated nutmeg. Simmer for three minutes, then add the faggots and simmer for a further ten minutes.

Spoon in the crème fraîche, season with salt and pepper and serve.

BLACK PUDDING WITH APPLE & FIG

Fruit goes terribly well with black pudding – the acidity of the fruit cuts through the unctuousness of the pudding to delightful effect. This starter is as visually appealing as it is tasty.

––––––––––––––––––––

Slice the apple and gently fry it with the onion in the butter, sugar and vinegar for 20 minutes until gooey and caramelised. Add the mustard and double cream, then decant into a small bowl.

Wipe the pan clean and pour in the olive oil. Fry the black pudding over moderate heat for a couple of minutes on each side until crispy.

Place a scoop of onion and apple mix on each plate. Top with two slices of black pudding, laying a quarter of a fig on each slice, and serve.

SERVES 2

1 rosy apple (preferably Braeburn, Jonagold or Golden delicious – not Bramley; they fall apart)

1 red onion, peeled and sliced

1 tablespoon butter

2 teaspoons sugar

2 teaspoons cider vinegar

1 teaspoon Dijon mustard

1 tablespoon double cream

1 tablespoon olive oil

4 slices black pudding

1 ripe fig, quartered

FISH & VEGGIE SAUSAGES

There is no escaping the fact that sausages are associated with meat in most people's minds, but it would be a great mistake to think that the story ends there. When all is said and done, a sausage is something encased in something else and there is no law that states that either of the somethings must come from animals. Writing this chapter and eating the results has been a revelation to your thoroughly carnivorous authors. The late Linda McCartney had a point: vegetarian sausages can be just as good as meat-based ones. The operative word is succulence. Sealing fish, mushrooms or vegetables in a casing guarantees this quality in abundance. The only price vegetarians have to pay is that cellulose skins are not suitable for frying.

SMOKED MACKEREL BOUDIN

SERVES 4–6

750g smoked mackerel, skin
removed, broken into pieces

50g flat leaf parsley

250g crème fraîche

5g white pepper

5g salt

3 large eggs

50g breadcrumbs

1.5m collagen or hog casings

2 teaspoons butter (for frying
the sausages)

Finely puréed mackerel sets into a beautiful paté in these simple
sausages. You can make them with either collagen or natural casings.
Serve the boudin with horseradish sauce and a beetroot salad.

Heat up a large pan of water.

Blend together the smoked mackerel, parsley, crème fraîche, pepper,
salt, eggs and breadcrumbs in a food-processor until smooth, then stuff
them into your casings. Tie off well and twist into sausages.

Blanch the boudins at 80–85°C for 20 minutes if you are using collagen
casings, or 30 minutes for hog ones. Remove the sausages from the pan,
chill them in cool running water and set aside. You can store them in the
refrigerator for up to three days, or you can freeze them until you need
them (but do not freeze for longer than six months).

If you've made your boudins in advance, you will need to defrost them,
if frozen, and reheat them before serving. If they have collagen casings,
gently heat them in water for ten minutes. If you used hog casings, fry
them very slowly in 2 teaspoons butter for around 20 minutes.

Serve with horseradish sauce and a crunchy salad with grated raw
beetroot and pea shoots or lambs lettuce.

TOFU SAUSAGES WITH SHIITAKE MUSHROOMS

MAKES 20–25 CHIPOLATA-SIZED SAUSAGES

100g sesame seeds

75g coriander, chopped

200g shiitake mushrooms, chopped

100g spring onions, chopped

500g fresh tofu, diced

50g ginger, finely chopped

50g miso paste

100ml teriyaki sauce

50ml sesame oil

50ml vegetable oil

500g cooked Thai sticky (glutinous) rice

small spool of sheep casings or cellulose casings

2 teaspoons sunflower oil (for frying the sausages)

Not being vegetarians, we make these splendid sausages with sheep casings. If this doesn't appeal, you can use cellulose skins, but then you'll have to warm up the sausages by boiling rather than frying them.

Dry-fry the sesame seeds gently for ten minutes, tossing them frequently, until golden brown.

Combine all the ingredients bar the casings in a large bowl and mix until mushy. You can either use a spoon or your fingers.

Fill into your chosen casings and tie off into chipolata-length sausages.

Simmer the sausages at 70–80°C for 40 minutes. Don't let the water temperature get any higher or the casings may split.

Cool the sausages under cold water. They will keep in the refrigerator for up to five days, or in the freezer for up to six months.

When the time comes to eat them, defrost them if frozen and fry them very gently in the oil in a non-stick pan until browned (if you made them with sheep casings) or simmer them until warmed through (if you used cellulose casings).

Serve with stir-fried Chinese greens.

BACALAO & PARSLEY SAUSAGES

Bacalao is salted cod, which has to be soaked prior to use. As with our Tofu Sausages with Shiitake Mushrooms (see opposite), you can use either sheep or cellulose casings, but if you go for the latter, you won't be able to fry them ahead of serving. You'll have to blanch them instead.

■ ■ ■ ■ ■ ■ ■ ■ ■ ■ ■ ■ ■ ■ ■ ■

Gently fry the bacalao, shallots and garlic in the olive oil for 15 minutes, stirring frequently.

Transfer to your food-processor along with the flat leaf parsley, eggs, pimenton, crème fraîche and potatoes. Pulse about ten times until mixed.

Fill into your chosen casings and tie off into chipolata-length sausages.

Simmer the sausages at 70–80°C for 40 minutes. Don't let the water temperature get any higher or the casings may split.

Cool the sausages under cold water. They will keep in the fridge for up to five days, or in the freezer for up to six months.

When you're ready to eat them, fry them very gently in the butter in a non-stick pan until browned (if you made them with sheep casings) or simmer them until warmed through (if you used cellulose casings).

Serve with roasted red peppers, a drizzle of good olive oil and a hunk of crusty bread.

MAKES 20–25 CHIPOLATA-SIZED SAUSAGES

300g bacalao, filleted, chopped and soaked in plenty of cold water overnight

150g shallots, finely chopped

15g garlic, peeled and finely chopped

75ml olive oil

30g flat leaf parsley

4 large eggs

5g ground Pimenton de la Vera (sweet, smoky Spanish paprika)

150g crème fraîche

700g potatoes, soft boiled and drained

small spool of sheep casings or cellulose casings

2 teaspoons butter (for frying the sausages)

MUSHROOM SAUSAGES WITH CAVOLO NERO & POTATOES

SERVES 4

The Sausages

500g white or brown mushrooms,
100g fresh shiitake mushrooms and
10g dried porcini (ceps) powder

2 medium red onions, peeled

15g garlic, peeled and chopped

50g capers, chopped

150g freshly blended breadcrumbs

100g roughly grated Parmesan

5g salt and 5g black pepper

25g flat leaf parsley, chopped

200g crème fraîche

100ml olive oil

small spool of collagen or
cellulose casings

The Accompaniments

6 medium potatoes, unpeeled, diced

few sprigs rosemary

750g cavolo nero

2 garlic cloves, peeled and chopped

2 pinches dried red chilli flakes

olive oil

The luxurious sausages at the heart of this dish are flavoured with three kinds of mushroom, including powdered porcini, which imparts an earthy depth. They are best made with collagen or cellulose casings; these rupture easily in the frying pan so you are better off blanching them.

Chop or blend the mushrooms and onions together until finely diced, then fry in the olive oil for around 30 minutes, stirring frequently, until the juices have evaporated.

Transfer the mushroom and onion mixture to a large bowl and thoroughly mix in the rest of the ingredients.

Fill the stuffing into collagen casings and twist into about 20 sausages that are each roughly 15cm long. Take care to tie them off well – given the slightest opportunity they will spurt out their contents.

Blanch the sausages in water heated to 80–85°C (any hotter and the casings will split) for 15 minutes. (If you don't plan to eat them immediately, cool them down in cold running water and store in the refrigerator for up to five days, or in the freezer for up to four months, then, when you're ready to eat them, defrost if frozen and simmer for about 5 minutes until warmed through.)

Meanwhile, boil the diced potatoes for 15 minutes until soft. After draining, fry them with the rosemary in 50ml olive oil over moderate heat, stirring frequently.

Remove the spines from the cavolo nero and discard. Roughly chop the leaves. Stir-fry the cavolo nero with the garlic and chilli flakes in enough oil to cover the bottom of your pan or wok. The cabbage needs to be cooked hard for a few minutes and stirred vigorously until it has wilted.

Serve everything together on a large platter.

GLAMORGAN SAUSAGE WITH CREAMY BABY SPINACH

Purists might say that Glamorgan sausage is no more sausage than Bombay Duck is duck or aubergine caviar the eggs of sturgeon. Never mind. These cheesy delights are well worth experimenting with. They can be shallow-fried in butter or oil or you can bake them. If you opt for the latter, drizzle a little oil over them before they go in the oven to help them cook evenly.

Put the cheese, half the breadcrumbs, the leek, parsley, thyme, eggs, Dijon mustard and half of the double cream into a large bowl. Season with the salt and white pepper, then roll up your sleeves and mix everything together.

Shape the mixture into small sausages and roll them in the remaining breadcrumbs.

Gently fry the sausages in a touch of olive oil until golden brown. Be careful with them as they are fragile.

While the sausages are frying, pour a dab of olive oil into a large wok or saucepan and place over moderate heat. Wilt the spinach, stirring constantly, then season with salt, pepper and finely grated nutmeg. Finally, stir in the remaining cream and serve alongside the piping hot Glamorgan sausages.

SERVES 4–6

The Sausages

250g Caerphilly cheese, finely grated

200g fresh white breadcrumbs

½ medium leek, finely chopped

2 tablespoons chopped flat leaf parsley

1 sprig thyme, chopped

2 eggs

2 heaped teaspoons Dijon mustard

200ml double cream

1 teaspoon salt

½ teaspoon ground white pepper

olive oil

The Spinach

olive oil

500g baby leaf spinach

¼ nutmeg, freshly grated

salt and freshly ground black pepper

FISHCAKE SAUSAGES

These charming little sausages are always a hit with small children. You can make them with most kinds of fish fillet. Haddock works well, so does salmon.

—————————————————————

Thoroughly mash together all the ingredients, bar the casings, in a large bowl. Don't be tempted to blend them in a food-processor as you want the sausages to have a bit of texture.

Fill the mixture into collagen casings and tie off into 15cm links – you should have approximately 24 sausages.

Blanch the sausages in water heated to 80–85°C for 20 minutes (if you try to fry them they will burst).

Either serve the fishcake sausages immediately, perhaps accompanied by asparagus tips or peas, or cool them down in cold running water. They will keep in the fridge for up to three days or in the freezer for up to four months.

To reheat the sausages, simmer them gently in water heated to around 80°C for ten minutes.

SERVES 4

500g skinless fish fillet, broken into small pieces

500g potatoes, peeled, sliced and boiled for 20 minutes until soft

100g fresh breadcrumbs

150ml double cream

2 eggs

50g capers, chopped

6 spring onions, finely sliced

5g salt

3g white pepper

small spool of collagen casings

SAUSAGES A-Z

Andouille (France) Large sausages stuffed with, as well as encased by, various parts of the digestive tract of pigs, or less often veal. Often smoked, they are an acquired taste and sometimes stink to high heaven.

Andouille (USA) A heavily smoked pork and garlic sausage flavoured with cayenne pepper. Used extensively in the Cajun cooking of Louisiana, for example in gumbos and jambalayas. Has none of the challenging features of French andouilles.

Andouillette Smaller version of andouille.

Bierwurst A precooked smoked German sausage made from beef and pork and flavoured with garlic and mustard seeds. Somewhat like salami in appearance. Doesn't contain beer but goes very well with chilled lager.

Black pudding A British blood sausage containing a high proportion of oatmeal.

Bockwurst A Frankfurter-like sausage invented by R. Scholtz of Berlin in 1889. Usually smoked and flavoured with paprika.

Boerwors The definitive South African sausage, made from coarsely cut pork, beef or both. The name means 'farmer's sausage'. It is flavoured with copious quantities of ground coriander and other spices and contains vinegar.

Bologna A large smoked American sausage made of finely ground beef, pork, veal or a mixture. Descended from the infinitely superior mortadella, it is known as 'baloney' in some parts of the US, which indicates its low culinary status.

Boudin blanc A delectable precooked French sausage containing cream, eggs and finely minced pork or chicken. Particularly popular around Christmas.

Boudin noir A cereal-free French blood sausage containing pork offal and head meat in addition to pig's blood.

Bratwurst A finely minced German sausage usually made from pork. The city of Nuremberg is famous for its bratwurst.

Butifarra A term covering a wide range of Catalan fresh pork sausages. Butifarra negra contains blood and mint as well as pork meat.

Cambridge An excellent fresh sausage from the university town spiced with nutmeg and sometimes ginger.

Cervelat The national sausage of Switzerland, made with emulsified pork and beef and lightly smoked. Also popular in Germany. The name comes from cervelle, the French for 'brains', which used to be one of the key ingredients.

Chaurice Creole/Cajun version of chorizo.

Chipolata Small pork sausage, bizarrely deriving its name from cipolla, the Italian for onion (it doesn't contain any).

Chorizo A family of Spanish and Latin American sausages whose common denominator is that they are made with pork and pimentón (paprika). Some are fresh, some cured. Mexican chorizo is particularly spicy as it contains red chillies.

Chouriço Portuguese version of chorizo made with pork cured in brine.

Cotechino A fat (and fatty) pork-based Italian sausage traditionally eaten with lentils on New Year's Eve. Needs to be boiled before consumption.

Crepinette The French equivalent of a faggot, consisting of sausage meat wrapped in caul fat.

Cumberland A coarsely minced pork sausage traditionally formed into long, unbroken coils.

Drisheen Irish black pudding made with sheep's blood in Limerick, pig's blood in Cork and Kerry and goose blood in Clare.

Extrawurst A German/Austrian precooked sausage made from beef, pork or a combination of the two and usually eaten cold. The term 'extrawurst' is also used of people with particularly high opinions of themselves.

Faggots British pork sausage meat parcels wrapped in caul fat. They often but not always contain offal.

Figatello Corsican sausage made with lamb's liver.

Frankfurter Arguably the world's most popular sausage. Usually made with pork in Germany and beef in the USA.

Fuet A thin pure pork salami from Catalunya. The name means 'whip'.

Gänseleberwurst A luxurious German sausage made from goose liver and truffles.

Garlic sausage In Britain at least, a large steam cooked sausage made from cured pork, garlic and spices. Usually sliced and eaten cold.

Glamorgan A Welsh vegetarian sausage made with Caerphilly cheese and encased in breadcrumbs rather than a sausage skin.

Gloucester A fresh pork sausage flavoured with sage and other herbs, traditionally made with meat from the Gloucester Old Spot pig.

Goteborg Hard smoked Swedish sausage made from beef and pork in a 3 to 1 ratio.

Gyulai Mildly smoked Hungarian sausage made with pork and sweet peppers.

Haggis The 'chieftain o' the puddin' race', traditionally made with sheep's lungs, liver and spleen plus oatmeal and onions. Traditionally sown into a sheep's stomach, it is now usually stuffed into beef bungs.

Hammelwurst A German mutton sausage.

Jésus A huge French salami.

Kabanos A thin, smoked Polish sausage made from densely packed pork and often flavoured with caraway seeds.

Kielbasa In its native Polish, the word kielbasa just means 'sausage'. In the USA, the term denotes a smoked precooked sausage made with pork, garlic and marjoram.

Kindziuk/Skilandis Cold smoked pork based Lithuanian sausage containing pure alcohol.

Knackwurst/Knockwurst A short, thick precooked German sausage made with beef, pork or a mixture of both.

Knockpølse The Danish equivalent of knackwurst.

Kosher salami Made with beef rather than pork for obvious reasons.

Krakowska A lean, close textured smoked Polish sausage originally from the city of Krakow.

Landjäger A square Swabian sausage made with beef, caraway and garlic and cold smoked.

Lap cheong A hard, air dried Chinese pork sausage with a sweet flavour. The name literally means 'waxed intestine'.

Leberwurst Smooth, precooked spreadable liver based sausage from Germany. Pig's liver usually accounts for about 20 per cent of its weight. The rest is made up of lean and fat pork, onions and various spices.

Lincolnshire Coarsely ground fresh pork sausage flavoured with sage.

Linguica Portuguese/Brazilian pork sausage made with garlic, paprika and onion. Usually smoked and needs to be cooked before consumption.

Longaniza Spanish cured sausage similar to chorizo. Very popular in Latin America and the Philippines. The Argentinian version is flavoured with aniseed.

Loukanika Fresh Greek pork or lamb sausage distinctively flavoured with red wine and orange peel.

Lucanian Ancient Roman fresh pork sausage described by the 4th Century cookery writer Apicius. Key ingredients include crushed almonds and garum, a condiment made from fermented fish.

Mazzafegato Pork liver sausage from Norcia in Italy containing pine kernels, fennel and garlic.

Medwurst Smoked semi-dry pork sausage from Sweden containing potatoes.

Merguez Spicy red North African sausage made from lamb or beef but never pork. Excellent with couscous.

Mettwurst Cold smoked German sausage usually made from pure pork but sometimes incorporating veal and/or beef. Some versions are soft and spreadable, others are harder.

Morcilla Spanish blood sausage made with cooked rice.

Mortadella Huge, classic precooked sausage from Bologna, made with finely ground pork and cubed fat in a ratio of 7 to 3. Sometimes studded with pistachio nuts and flavoured with wine, it always contains garlic and is usually eaten in thin slices.

Newmarket Johnny's uncle would never speak to him again if we didn't include this excellent herby pork sausage from Suffolk. There are two versions, reflecting the fact that two different butchers claim possession of the 'authentic' recipe. One contains breadcrumbs, the other rusk.

Nham Fermented Thai pork sausage containing cooked rice, garlic and fiery chillies.

Oyster sausage Very popular in Victorian times, oyster sausages contain veal or pork in addition to the bivalve that gives them their name.

Pepperoni Spelled 'peperone' in its native Italy, this spicy, cured salami-like sausage is one of the world's favourite pizza toppings. It is made with a mixture of beef and pork and gets its kick from hot red peppers.

Polish smoked Generic term for hot smoked pork sausages from guess where, Poland.

Reindyrpølse Norwegian reindeer sausage.

Rindswurst Precooked beef sausage from Frankfurt, which the locals tend to eat in greater quantities than the more famous pork sausage named after their city (see Germany feature, page 90).

Rookwurst A spicy Dutch smoked sausage featured in the 'How to Smoke Sausages' section of the introductory chapter of this book.

Rosette A salami from the Lyon region of France.

Salami Any member of a vast family of fermented sausages made with raw meat distinctively interspersed with cubes of back fat. Some of the best known varieties include:
Danish Bright pink variety made in enormous quantities for export. The Danes have been making salami since the Middle Ages.
Felino Pure pork plus wine and garlic
Finocchiona Made with fennel.
Fiorentino Usually made with pure pork and often includes larger pieces of lean meat among the fat and finely ground pork.
Hungarian, aka Pick Arguably the finest salami in the world, 'Pick' is made from pure pork and is lightly smoked before a long period of curing. The salamis were originally made with donkey meat but there weren't enough donkeys in the country to meet demand.
Milanese A finely textured salami made with pork and beef or veal flavoured with garlic and whole white peppercorns.
Napolitano A feisty pork and beef based salami flavoured with hot red peppers.
Nola Unlike most Italian salamis, this variety is smoked.

Salchichas Fresh Spanish sausages.

Salchichon de Vic A kind of cross between salami and cured chorizo made in the Catalunyan city of Vic.

Salsiccie Robust Fresh Italian pork sausages.

Saucisse Fresh French sausages, available in almost infinite varieties.

Saucisson Cured French sausages. The most famous is probably saucisson sec, which is a simple, quick cured salami made from pure pork.

Saveloy A bright red emulsified sausage sold from the counters of British fish and chip shops.

Schinkenwurst/Shinkenplockwurst Smoked sausage made in Westphalia in Germany from flaked ham studded with largish cubes of back fat.

Sheftalia Cypriot pork or lamb sausage flavoured with parsley and onion and wrapped in caul fat. For maximum authenticity and flavour, sheftalia should be barbecued.

Soppressata A variety of salami made in the Southern Italian provinces of Calabria, Puglia and Basilicato. Usually pressed flat during the maturing phase and heavily flavoured with garlic.

Sucuk Lean fermented beef and lamb sausage from Turkey.

Summer sausage Fermented, salami-style sausage from the USA. Usually made from a mixture of pork and beef, it is often smoked. It derives its name from the fact it is ready to eat in the summer, not because it is made in that season. It is traditionally made in autumn.

Teewurst Soft, spreadable uncooked German sausage made from two parts pork and or beef and one part bacon fat. After being stuffed into casings, the sausages are smoked over beechwood and hung to mature for a week to ten days. Teewurst derives its name from the fact that it is traditionally consumed at tea time.

Thuringer Fresh grilling sausage from the German state of Thuringia, made with finely ground meat flavoured with garlic, caraway and marjoram. By law, German fresh sausages must be sold on the day they are made.

Toulouse A coarse fresh sausage from South West France made with pork belly, red wine, garlic and nutmeg. Toulouse sausages are an essential ingredient in cassoulet.

Weisswurst Emulsified Bavarian sausage made from finely minced veal or pork and flavoured with parsley. Weisswurst are highly perishable. Residents of Munich have a phobia about eating them after the noon bells chime.

White pudding British sausage usually based on shredded pork or chicken and invariably containing oatmeal and suet. Fried slices of White Pudding are an integral part of a proper Irish breakfast. Scottish White Pudding, also known as Mealy Pudding, sometimes doesn't contain any meat at all.

Wiejska A lightly smoked, precooked Polish sausage. Wiejska means 'rural'.

Wienerwurst Alternative name for Frankfurter often corrupted to 'Wienie' in the USA.

Zampone Similar to a Cotechino but with the distinctive feature of being encased in a boned-out pig's trotter.

INDEX

ancho salami 21
andouille sausages 188
  crispy andouille with 5-spice 164
andouillettes 161, 188
apples 51, 64, 175
artichoke salad with salami, walnuts & Parmesan 120
aubergine & salami bake 126

bacalao & parsley sausages 181
baked Toulouse sausage with sauerkraut & apples 51
Baradieu Farm, France 52–55
Basque sausage with oysters 61
beans
  borlotti beans with fennel & salami 123
  sausage with home-cooked spicy beans 38
  Toulouse sausage & bean cassoulet 57
  Toulouse sausages with duck breast & butter beans 58
beer 88
black pudding 52, 188
  black pudding with apple & fig 175
  black pudding with cauliflower, topped with roasted hazelnuts 163
blood puddings 161
blood sausages 28–29
boudin blanc 6, 10, 22, 75, 188
  boudin blanc with crushed potatoes & caramelised red onions 86
  boudin blanc with morels in a creamy sauce 85
boudin noir 52, 188
bratwurst 90, 188
  bratwurst cooked in beer 88
Breton sausage & white wine potée 89
brioche 117

cabbage
  kielbasa Krakowska with red cabbage & caraway 107
  smoked sausage choucroute 101
caraway 8, 107

carrots
  venison sausage with honey glazed carrots 72
Casa Riera Ordeix, Spain 132–135
casings 13
cauliflower 163
cavolo nero 182
cheese
  artichoke salad with salami, walnuts & Parmesan 120
  chorizo & goat's cheese tart 137
  Frankfurters with petit pois & melting cheese 80
  ham and parsley sausages with melted cheese & leeks 36
  salami in brioche with Gruyère 117
  saucisse de Montbéliard with fennel & melted cheese 111
  sautéed sausages with sweet potato, goat's cheese & parsley 34
  Swiss chard baked with Frankfurters & Gruyère 99
  tomatoes stuffed with green olives, salami & Parmesan 130
  Vienna macaroni cheese 109
Chinese sausages 139, 140
chipolatas 188
  Nick's chipolatas 16
  sweet & sour sausages 70
chorizo 6, 18–19, 115, 188
  chorizo & goat's cheese tart 137
  chorizo & spinach soup 131
  chorizo baked with apple & red onion 64
  chorizo dog 152
  chorizo paella with seafood 67
  chorizo ravioli with parsley sauce 153
  chorizo with squid 65
  fresh chorizo 17
  huevos rancheros with chorizo 68
corn dogs 150
couscous with merguez 62
crème fraîche 48, 76
crepinettes 161, 188
  crepinettes with spinach & roasted almonds 172

Cumberland sausages 10, 16, 40, 188
cumin sausages 16
cured sausages 10, 18–21, 115
curing salts 13
currywurst with chips 82

duck
  Toulouse sausages with duck breast & butter beans 58

eggs 8
  huevos rancheros with chorizo 68
  Scotch eggs 156
equipment 12–13

faggots 188
  faggot & root vegetable stew 174
fennel 8
  borlotti beans with fennel & salami 123
  minestrone with fennel salami 129
  saucisse de Montbéliard with fennel & melted cheese 111
figs 175
fish sausages 10
  fishcake sausages 187
  smoked mackerel boudin 178
fougasse, salami & olive oil 125
Frankfurters 10, 24, 75, 90, 93, 188
  currywurst with chips 82
  Frankfurters with petit pois & melting cheese 80
  potato salad with grilled Frankfurters 78
fresh sausages 10, 14–17, 31

garlic
  roasted vegetables with garlic & smoked sausage 113
  wiejska with roasted garlic mash 102
Ginger Pig, England 40, 52
Glamorgan sausages 189
  Glamorgan sausages with creamy baby spinach 185
goose with veal stuffing 158
Gref-Völsings, Germany 90–93

haggis 6, 161, 166–168, 189
  haggis, neeps & tatties 171
ham 8
  ham and parsley sausages with melted cheese & leeks 36
  herby sausage dumplings in root vegetable stew 145
hotdogs 6
  stuffed hotdogs 112
hotpot of rookwurst & kale 94
huevos rancheros with chorizo 68
hygiene 12, 13
hygrometer 13

Italian sausage with tomato & sage sauce 122

kabanos 20, 189
kale 94
kielbasa 189
  kielbasa Krakowska with red cabbage & caraway 107
  kielbasa with pierogi 108
knackwurst 25, 189
  knackwurst with five spice 105

lap cheong 6, 189
leberwurst 90, 189
leeks
  ham and parsley sausages with melted cheese & leeks 36
lentils
  sausage and puy lentil stew 43
Lincolnshire sausages 10, 189
luxury veal sausages 23

macaroni cheese 109
making your own sausages 12–13
  blood sausages 28–29
  cured sausages 18–21
  fresh sausages 14–17
  precooked sausages 22–25
  smoked sausages 26–27
McSween, Scotland 166–168
merguez 17, 31, 189
  merguez with couscous 62
Milano salami 21
mincer 12
minestrone with fennel salami 129
morcilla 29, 189

mushrooms
boudin blanc with morels in a creamy sauce 85
mushroom sausages with cavolo nero & potatoes 182
paysanne sausage with ceps & root vegetables 49
tofu sausages with shiitake mushrooms 180
veal sausage schnitzel with mushroom sauce 81
mustard 48

Nick's chipolatas 16
noodles
weisswurst with creamy spaetzle 76
nuts 120, 162, 172

olives 130
onions
boudin blanc with crushed potatoes & caramelised red onions 86
chorizo baked with apple & red onion 64
sausage rolls with onion confit 154
oysters
Basque sausage with oysters 61
oyster sausages 189

parsley 34, 36, 153, 181
pasta with wild boar sausages 71
paysanne sausages 15
paysanne poached with spinach, potatoes, mustard & crème fraîche 48
paysanne sausage with ceps & root vegetables 49
peas
Frankfurters with petit pois & melting cheese 80
pepperoni 8, 189
pierogi with kielbasa 108
pigs 11, 32, 40
pork belly with red wine & cured sausage 119
pork loin with rustic sausage stuffing 153
potatoes
boudin blanc with crushed potatoes & caramelised red onions 86
haggis, neeps & tatties 171
mushroom sausages with cavolo nero & potatoes 182

paysanne poached with spinach, potatoes, mustard & crème fraîche 48
potato salad with grilled Frankfurters 78
sausage hotpot with Worcestershire sauce 44
warm salad with sauté potatoes & black pudding 165
wiejska with roasted garlic mash 102
prawns
chorizo paella with seafood 67
precooked sausages 10, 22–25, 75

rindswurst 90–93, 190
roasted goose with veal stuffing 158
roasted vegetables with garlic & smoked sausage 113
rookwurst 190
hotpot of rookwurst & kale 94
smoked rookwurst 27

sage 122
salami 6, 8, 21, 115, 189, 190
artichoke salad with salami, walnuts & Parmesan 120
borlotti beans with fennel & salami 123
minestrone with fennel salami 129
salami & aubergine bake 126
salami & olive oil fougasse 125
salami in brioche with Gruyère 117
tomatoes stuffed with green olives, salami & Parmesan 130
salchichon 8, 190
salchichon de Vic 132–135, 190
salchichon salad with baked cherry tomatoes 118
tortilla with salchichon 138
salsiccie 8, 190
saucisses 52, 190
saucisse de Montbéliard with fennel & melted cheese 111
saucissons 8, 52, 190
sauerkraut
baked Toulouse sausage with sauerkraut & apples 51
sausage & puy lentil stew 43
sausage cannelloni 148–149
sausage hotpot with Worcestershire sauce 44
sausage meat 10, 143
sausage pasties 146

sausage pot au feu with garden veg 37
sausage rolls with onion confit 154
sausage stuffer 12
sausage with home-cooked spicy beans 38
sausages poached in red wine & thyme 59
sautéed sausages with sweet potato, goat's cheese & parsley 34
saveloys 10, 25, 75, 190
saveloy & vegetable tempura 96
Scotch eggs 156
sesame stew with Chinese sausages 140
skinless sausages 10, 143
slow-cooked pork belly with red wine & cured sausage 119
smoked mackerel boudin 178
smoked sausages 26–27
roasted vegetables with garlic & smoked sausage 113
smoked sausage choucroute 101
spices
crispy andouille with 5-spice 164
knackwurst with five spice 105
spinach
chorizo & spinach soup 131
crepinettes with spinach & roasted almonds 172
Glamorgan sausages with creamy baby spinach 185
paysanne poached with spinach, potatoes, mustard & crème fraîche 48
squid
chorizo paella with seafood 67
chorizo with squid 65
starter culture 13
stir-fried Chinese sausages 139
sweet & sour sausages 70
sweet potatoes
sautéed sausages with sweet potato, goat's cheese & parsley 34
Swiss chard baked with Frankfurters & Gruyère 99

thermometer 13
thyme 59
toad in the hole 47
tofu sausages with shiitake mushrooms 180

tomatoes
Italian sausage with tomato & sage sauce 122
salchichon salad with baked cherry tomatoes 118
tomatoes stuffed with green olives, salami & Parmesan 130
tortilla with salchichon 138
Toulouse sausages 10, 17, 31, 40, 52, 190
baked Toulouse sausage with sauerkraut & apples 51
Toulouse sausage & bean cassoulet 57
Toulouse sausages with duck breast & butter beans 58

veal
luxury veal sausages 23
roasted goose with veal stuffing 158
veal sausage schnitzel with mushroom sauce 81
vegetable sausages 10
vegetables
faggot & root vegetable stew 174
herby sausage dumplings in root vegetable stew 145
paysanne sausage with ceps & root vegetables 49
roasted vegetables with garlic & smoked sausage 113
sausage pot au feu with garden veg 37
saveloy & vegetable tempura 96
venison sausages 17
venison sausage with honey-glazed carrots 72
Vienna macaroni cheese 109

warm salad with sauté potatoes & black pudding 165
weisswurst 24, 90, 190
weisswurst with creamy spaetzle 76
wiejska 10, 25, 190
wiejska with roasted garlic mash 102
Wienerwurst 90, 190
wild boar sausages 71
wine 59, 89, 119
Worcestershire sauce 44